Bill W...
MOUNTAIN
MEN

Adventures of Arizona's buckskin trail riders

by Thomas E. Way

Golden West Publishers

COVER DESIGN: Bruce Robert Fischer

PHOTO CREDITS: front and back cover photos and pages 31, 38, 56, 80, 95/Phoenix Jaycees; inside front cover and pages 8, 26, 40, 70, 74, 99, 105, 109, 122/C. M. Whitaker; pages 14, 116, 118, 121/Thomas E. Way; pages 18, 24, 107/ Elmer Hubbard; pages 35, 61/Phoenix Gazette; page 43/Ft. Madison Democrat; page 46/Washington Star; page 48/U.S. Government; pages 50, 62, 123/ Bill Nixon; page 80/Ralph Painter; page 91/The Smoki; page 101/Earl's Camera Shop; page 102/ Good Samaritan Hospital; page 103/Dr. George H. Wood. Photos not otherwise credited were taken by one of the following: Bill Nixon, Elmer Hubbard, Ralph Painter, C. M. Whitaker and Bob Ziriax.

Library of Congress Cataloging-in-Publication Data

Way, Thomas E.
    Bill Williams' Mountain Men.

    Includes index.
    1. Bill Williams' Mountain Men (Group) 2. Williams, Bill, 1787-1849. 3. Frontier and pioneer life--Arizona. 4. Arizona--Social life and customs. I. Title.
F811.W36 1987   979.1'00886391   87-11884
ISBN 0-914846-30-2

Printed in the United States of America

Golden West Publishers
4113 N. Longview Ave.
Phoenix, AZ 85014, USA
  (602) 265-4392

Contents

Foreword

The buckskin-clad mountain men were a hardy group who forsook civilization for the lonely life of a trapper on the raw, new western frontier. They literally took their lives in their hands and braved Indians, grizzlies and worse—the cold relentless winters of the vast unexplored mountain wilderness. Theirs was, of necessity, a hard life, for only the virgin territory beyond civilization offered the prime beaver pelts, much in demand by eastern fur markets.

Many were squawmen. Some were outcasts sought by minions of the law. Some chose this lonely existence for love of exploration. Some to be near God. Bill Williams was of the latter stock. Having been a preacher, he always carried a bible on his forays in the wilds.

These mountain men were a breed of their own; different from other frontiersmen. They sometimes "counted *coup*" by taking the scalps of their enemies and were always ready to do battle to protect their lives and interests in the never-ending struggle against man and the elements. The West has never produced a more self-subsistent clan of rugged individualists.

They were in Northern Arizona Territory as early as the 1820's. James Ohio Pattie led a party up the San Francisco River (now known as the Verde) in search of beaver in 1824. He wrote of the then unnamed mountain (Bill Williams) that stood out as a "landmark visible for many miles in all directions." Bill Williams, Antoine Leroux and other mountain men spoke of this area in glowing terms, when they met at rendezvous at Taos.

Who in his right mind would have any desire to revert to a life filled with such dangers as were faced daily by these mountain men?

In an effort to rejuvenate that segment of Arizoniana, a group of Williams, Arizona, residents indulged what started as wishful thinking, turning it into a challenge of adventure resulting in the eventual organizing of the Bill Williams Mountain Men. With few changes—members dropping out and new members added—

the group is still going strong after more than thirty-two years. Only two of the charter members—Denton Dean and Bill Lilly—are still active in the organization.

Time is getting away from us. Six charter members and many of those who joined later have (as of 1986) taken that lonely trail over the Great Divide where they are scouting new trails in the land of plenty and waiting for us to join them in another rendezvous.

The horseback riding I did was on an occasional basis. As the need arose I drove the refreshment truck—cook truck—the hay, grain or bedroll truck. I spent a lot of time aiding and abetting the various cooks and doing other camp chores. We had a different cook every year.

We all horsebacked it in the various parades. In later parades I was the wounded mountain man being hauled on the travois, where I had a worm's-eye view of the proceedings.

I was a member the first twelve years. I had made all twelve rendezvous trips, many parades and two inaugural trips to Washington, D.C. It was time to hang up the old "scalping knife" and retire the buckskins.

If this narrative brings nostalgic memories of back-country trails once explored and channels the mind into another imaginary rendezvous ride with the old gang, or perhaps rekindles a latent spark of adventure in others, my goal will have been achieved.

Happy trails.

T.E.W.

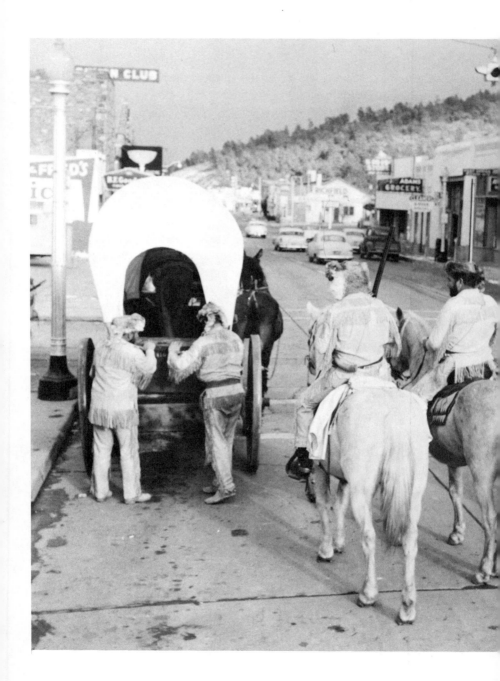

How It Started

to "perpetuate the lore, memory and romance . . ."

From the start the idea centered around a proposed horseback outing. I first heard of it in a wayside waterhole where thirsty wayfarers were wont to meet on occasion to discuss the day's events. That particular day the *piece de resistance* being bandied about was the forming of some sort of a riding club (horseback) which would alleviate the otherwise mundane daily existence of the average businessman for a brief time—to give him a chance to temporarily live in a fantasyland of pleasure; perhaps to re-enact a segment of particularly interesting history of the area.

Ideas were many and varied—make an overnight camping trip into the outback; an overnight trek could soon become a several day adventure; take guests along at so much per head; have a pack train haul supplies, bedding, etc.; make an annual affair of it. In the embryonic stages of growing pains one idea mushroomed and overflowed into another. A lot of ideas were mulled over and most of them were eventually discarded in an effort to sift the chaff from the wheat.

From these random brainstorms finally evolved an idea that seemed to bear fruit. Why not wear buckskin clothing like the old scouts and trail blazers? Why not name the group after the famous old mountain man who posthumously gave his name to the town and the mountain that stands guard nearby?

Who was this man?

William Sherley Williams was born January 3, 1787 in Rutherford County, North Carolina. He died March 14, 1849, near the headwaters of the Rio Grande in Southern Colorado. Between those dates his travels covered much of the central and western states and territories. His adventures were many and he did "a heap of livin'," most of which is unrecorded, in the 62 years allotted to him.

On the day of their deaths, Bill Williams and Dr. Benjamin J. Kern, accompanied by "a few Mexicans", were searching for the hidden cache of the ill-fated Fremont Expedition of the previous winter (1848-49). This cache consisted of several packmule loads of surveying instruments, saddles and other baggage in addition to books and records of the expedition. These supplies had been hastily hidden somewhere in the deep snow along Del Norte, a tributary of the upper Rio Grande, when the expedition faced disaster after many of the group had frozen to death and the same fate faced the entire group.

Bill Williams was falsely accused by Col. Fremont of misdirecting the party and was blamed for causing the deaths of the group in the mountains of Southern Colorado. History has since vindicated Old Bill on that incident and placed the blame on Fremont himself.

Old Bill and Dr. Kern were shot and killed by a small party of warring Utes. The Mexicans were not harmed but were allowed to leave unhurt. They were the bearers of the tragic news to the outside world.

At the time of his death the Old Master Trapper's hair, once a fiery red, had turned grey and his once erect body was "somewhat bent". Surely nobody could ever get the drop on Old Bill in his prime. Maybe the Utes who did him in made a mistake, which might also explain the statement of a newspaperman of that time—

"It is likely the members of the band of Utes who killed Old Bill did not recognize him. Afterwards, when it was discovered who it was they had killed, he was given a chief's burial with all the accompanying pomp of the ceremony."

The same source further stated, "Thus died Bill Williams—a fair specimen of the old mountaineer—a set of men now nearly extinct; a set of men who possessed warm hearts, had noble purposes and as courageous spirits as could be found in any state or society. Rude and unpolished, but tender and true, firm in a fight, but gentle as a woman to misfortune and distress—true Paladins of the mountains and the plains."

With a predecessor like Old Bill to emulate, our search for a name for the newly-formed organization was over—we would be the Bill Williams Mountain Men.

Interest reached a peak when Rod Graves took the bull by the horns. Rod was a doer and a leader. The clarion call went out for any and all interested parties to attend a meeting to be held at Rod's Steak House after the close of business December 29, 1953.

Those present at that meeting were Thurman Mayes, John A. "Doc" Stewart, Verne Carothers, Paul Tissaw, Jake January, Ray Larson, Denton "Diz" Dean, Rodney "Rod" Graves, Louis Landry and Thomas E. "Spike" Way. By then our serious intent was obvious—we had a picture taken of those who showed up for the meeting. That was one of the first of several organizational meetings at which many gallons of coffee were consumed.

The *esprit de corps* was contagious. Bill Lilly, Fred Theroux, Ray Stewart, Ben Fillmore, Vance Miller, Gordon McDowell and Reuben Dial were there for subsequent meetings. A slate of officers was elected: Rod Graves, president; Paul Tissaw, vice-president and trail-boss; Denton Dean, secretary-treasurer; with a board of directors consisting of Thurman Mayes, Jake January and Vance Miller.

By then the various ideas had melded into one general plan that still needed the wrinkles ironed out. Rod had long since sent for and received a catalog from an outfit in the east that made buckskin uniforms for such organizations as this. We ordered our buckskins, made our own fur hats, belts and knives. We hired a lawyer, drew up our constitution and by-laws and were on our way toward being a full-fledged corporation. Our chosen name—"Bill Williams Mountain Men"—was registered with the Secretary of State.

This would be an organization based on a segment of our heritage; in effect, an adventure off the beaten path of other hackneyed trail rides in existence elsewhere. Based on the thought—"this is not just another trail ride for dudes"—we would perpetuate the lore, memory and romance of that

First organizational meeting in 1953 (l. to r.) Thurman Mayes, Dr. John Stewart, Verne Carothers, "Spike" Way, Paul Tissaw, Jake January, Ray Larson, Denton Dean, Rod Graves and Louis Landry.

intrepid group of mountain men, particularly Old Bill Williams. As near as possible we would emulate the costumes and customs of our predecessors. We would rendezvous in the spring, just as they did in the yesteryears of our history—a heritage we looked anxiously forward toward fulfilling. Our enthusiasm gathered momentum.

We were more than a hundred years too late to obtain advice from Old Bill, who had gone on before; consequently, considerable research was in order to obtain authentic information as to clothing, weapons, etc. of those we chose to emulate. The mountain men of old were primarily beaver trappers. Their scouting and trail blazing activities came later, when the advance of civilization surged westward—particularly, with the advent of the California gold rush in 1849.

The group was named for the mountain man who, more than any other, was directly involved in our local history. Old Bill Williams—itinerant preacher (when the spirit moved him), scalp hunter and scout (without peer), trail-blazer (extraordinary), horse thief (mediocre), and squawman (periodic), but above all else, a mountain man! Head and shoulders above others of his breed, "Old Lone Wolf" (he was known by many names, all descriptive of his actions) was at times an enemy of the Indians—at other times, their friend.

Through all the mystery surrounding this man of the frontier nothing stands out more clearly than his love of adventure and desire to be alone in the western country he liked. There were those mountain men who thought that Old Bill Williams' infatuation for the then unnamed mountain was so sincere that his ghost lurked in that vicinity after his death. It was one of his peers, Antoine Leroux, who suggested to cartographers of the Sitgreaves, mapping expedition in 1851, that they give the mountain his (Bill's) name. Leroux was a mountain man hired to guide and hunt for the Sitgreaves Expedition. When maps were later printed, the prominent landmark did indeed bear Old Bill's name.

The present day Bill Williams Mountain Men, in full regalia, assemble in the spring and ride horseback 186 miles in six days (more or less depending on the route followed) from Williams to rendezvous in Phoenix, camping each night along the trail. However, a concession to conformity with old-time custom is made; when off the beaten path in the back country, more comfortable clothing is substituted, as the ride is long and the modern day mountain men are not entirely accustomed to that somewhat primitive way of life.

In olden times in the spring, after the winter's trapping season, the mountain men secured the winter's cache of beaver hides on pack animals and took them to rendezvous where representatives of the fur companies were gathered.

The Rocky Mountain Fur Company and American Fur Company were probably the leaders in the field with an occasional buyer from the Canadian-based Hudson's Bay Company. However, this area was far afield from the usual base of Hudson's Bay operations.

There was often intense rivalry among the fur buyers. Beaver was especially valuable. Hatters in New York, London, Paris and other cultural centers required large quantities of beaver hides. Gentlemen of standing and culture required beaver hats. The higher one stood in the social register, the better the grade of fur used in making his hat. The coarse grade of fur on the back was one-, two- or three-X grade. Down the sides was four-or five-X. As the fur texture changed down the side and became progressively finer, the grade increased. The limited amount of soft "belly beaver" was 10-X or top grade and, of necessity, far more expensive.

To fill the needs of the hat market, the mountain men trapped far off the beaten path where winters were severe and long, where the element of cold weather produced prime fur. The popularity of the beaver hat continued for many years. Consequently, by the early 1840's, the beaver faced extinction as did the buffalo forty years later.

While at rendezvous, after the beaver pelts were sold, the mountain men repaired their traps and trappings and generally got ready for the next trapping season. They bought trinkets, beads, cooking utensils—in fact, anything the fur buyers had in stock. Very little money changed hands; trade was accomplished by barter of goods of some sort. The standard item of barter, aside from an occasional stolen horse or two, among the mountain men was beaver hides. These were traded for beads, trinkets, etc., which, in turn, were then traded by the mountain men in the friendly Indian camps at or near the rendezvous site.

The story went the rounds that an Indian near Bent's Fort once came into possession of an early-day version of a crank-operated egg beater. The tribal medicine man promptly confiscated the mysterious gadget and thereafter effected some remarkable cures within the tribe by churning the air about the patient's ears (or wherever the ailment was) with the egg beater. Fur buyers usually had an array of what would now be classified as junk, but at the time was a veritable treasure trove to the primitive Indian.

Squaws were adept at repairing or making new buckskin clothing; they had the leather and the time and, for a string of colorful beads or other trade goods in exchange for materials and labor, the mountain man's wardrobe was replenished.

On the way to rendezvous, the mountain man did not pass up the opportunity to steal a few ponies if opportunity afforded. These ponies came in handy for trade with the Indians. The ponies were ideal trading material in seeking the favors of the Indian maidens. A good pony was a guarantee of the favors of the camp's most attractive squaw—her father got the pony.

Rendezvous was also a time to cut loose and celebrate another successful trapping season. The fur buyers had brought along a generous supply of fire water for just such an occasion as that. By the time the mountain man left for another trapping season he was broke.

After rendezvous the fur buyers were, for the most part, happy; the Indians were happy; everyone was well pleased with the outcome of another rendezvous. Even the disgruntled mountain men were content with the way things turned out; but as they headed back to the mountains they vowed they would stay reasonably sober if they lived to attend next year's rendezvous and thus avoid the inevitable bad-booze-caused headache.

Chimney Rock (Bill Williams Monument)

When they left rendezvous the mountain men knew where and when next year's rendezvous would be held. For many years rendezvous was in the same place year after year. In later years this time-honored tradition was replaced by doing business at regularly established trading posts.

Our new organization would rendezvous as did the mountain men of another era. We would rendezvous in all our trappings in commemoration of the mountain men of olden times. Of course, there would be no beaver hides and hopefully no stolen ponies. As to the latter—we did come close one time, but therein lies a tale:

Through no fault of our own we came into temporary possession of an extra horse on one of our early trips. At the noon stop on this particular day, nose bags (called morells) of grain were hung on each horse as usual. The nose count revealed there was an extra horse in the bunch. There were always a few extra horses in case one went lame and had to be trailered out; then there were the pack horses and the ones used to haul the travois in the parade at the end of the trip. Another count showed there still was another horse that didn't belong in the herd.

It was discovered that whoever had been watching the gate at a ranch a couple miles back had let one of the rancher's horses slip through unnoticed with our group. Having a feed of grain, this horse was in no hurry to leave.

Paul Tissaw saved the day. He roped and led the stray horse out of the herd. "We don't need anyone accusing us of stealing horses," said Paul, as he started off in a high trot leading the horse back the two miles to his pasture. Paul retrieved the feed bag and rejoined the group—no sweat to an old hand like Paul.

Originally, the by-laws called for a rendezvous ride to be made each year; there was no set destination, just a ride of undetermined length or destination. That brought about the possible destination of Las Vegas, Nevada, among other ideas. Several years later (May 1959) an extracurricular ride, mostly by trailering the horses, was made to Las Vegas. We graced the Las Vegas Helldorado Days Parade and, as usual, were well received. This, however, did not replace the annual rendezvous ride which had been completed two months previous.

We were faced with the question—"where can a bunch of modern-day mountain men, who never saw a beaver hide, rendezvous?" How about the world-famous Grand Canyon? That sixty-mile journey would be a two or three day jaunt of easy riding for a bevy of tenderfeet. Most of us got on a horse about once a year. That word "tenderfeet" is a misnomer—that is not the part of the anatomy that gets the unaccustomed wear.

Somehow or other that destination (Grand Canyon) didn't arouse much interest. Although some of us in the organization were not exactly at home on the range, we had some members who were or had been genuine cowboys—we needed more than a two or three day ride. After all—the Canyon is in our front yard; we could see it any time.

The destination situation was settled when someone suggested that the J.C.'s in Phoenix were soon to host their annual World's Championship Rodeo. That would be much better, giving us close to a week on the trail. Phoenix was then and has since been the focal point of the Bill Williams Mountain Men's annual rendezvous ride.

Another by-law covered membership—"to qualify for membership a person must live in, or in the vicinity of Williams." That was defined to mean—"one who has a Williams mailing address."

The first rendezvous trip, in March 1954, was made by thirteen charter members—Rod Graves, Paul Tissaw, Denton "Diz" Dean, Jake January, Thurman Mayes, Louis Landry, Bill Lilly, Ben Fillmore, John Mills, Fred Theroux, Ray Stewart, Verne Carothers and T. E. "Spike" Way. Though there were few in that bunch who were not acquainted with a Dutch oven, inside and out, we hired a cook, Bob LeBlanc, and everyone pitched in to help him take care of camp chores.

The by-laws stated specifically that to be a full-fledged member of the club, that member must have completed a specified trip. The above thirteen members were deemed and/or have been generally acknowledged to be the co-founders and charter members of the Bill Williams Mountain Men, Inc. According to the by-laws, Dr. John A. "Doc" Stewart, not having made the initial trip, could not qualify as a charter member *per se,* but he was definitely a co-founder of the club. Thus we had fourteen members, thirteen of them being charter members. Others who attended some of the meetings could not spare the time from business or for some other reason were not on the trip; Gordon McDowell and Ray Larson did join a few years later.

Nobody worked harder than Doc Stewart to get the club organized and on the road. A tough run of luck, almost at the last minute, prevented him from making the first trip, but he kept in touch with the progress of our journey.

Doc and Verne Carothers were radio hams (licensed radio operators). They conversed nightly and thus kept us in touch with home and they with our goings-on. Doc suggested he could pass along to our families any news worthy of note—such as Indian attacks or if any of us were picked up for rustling horses, collecting scalps, etc. He could, he said—"report such activities to your wives, who are undoubtedly glad to be rid of you for a few days."

Our acceptance in Phoenix was beyond our fondest hopes. The J.C.'s and all of Phoenix welcomed us like long-lost brothers. The authenticity of our group and its clothing, trappings and mannerisms may best be attested by the fact that we won first prize in the "Best Mounted Group" division in the annual pre-rodeo parade in Phoenix that year and for many succeeding years thereafter.

A highlight of that initial rendezvous was, and still is an important part of the agenda: the visits to the various crippled children's hospitals to cheer up the kids. These kids anxiously look forward to these visitations. If their lives can be made a little happier with a cheery word and a look into the realm of the legendary storyland past, then the discomfort of a face full of whiskers and the rigors of the trail are a small price to pay for these bearded riders who temporarily shove back the pages of history to emerge from a vanished frontier.

We knew we had it made on that day in 1954; every time we

passed a bunch of kids, and later along the parade route in Phoenix, the kids broke into the song "Davy Crockett" every time they saw us and every time an announcer explained our group and where we were from. The exploits of Davy Crockett were the subject of a popular motion picture and TV series of that time. Davy Crockett was a "plainsman" who might be regarded as a "kissin' cousin" of the mountain man. There was a similarity of dress between the two types of frontiersman.

After the parade, an adult was heard to wonder aloud in a more earthy manner—"Where the hell is Williams?"

We were there to tell him.

Mountain Men assemble near Bill Williams Mountain.

The First Rendezvous
(1954)

red-carpet treatment in Phoenix

The charter members of the Bill Williams Mountain Men were of diversified backgrounds. Rod Graves was a restaurateur and cattle-rancher; Paul Tissaw, cattle rancher and lawman; Thurman Mayes, cowboy-foreman of Greenway Ranch; Jake January, cowboy and heavy equipment operator; Denton "Diz" Dean, tavern owner and carpenter; Bill Lilly, chef and carpenter; Louis Landry, teacher and welder; Ben Fillmore, filling station attendant; Fred Theroux, filling station owner and airplane A & E mechanic; Ray Stewart, motel owner; John Mills, restaurant owner and cook; Verne Carothers, Valle Airport Manager (TWA); and Thomas E. "Spike" Way, J. P./Magistrate.

Shortly after daybreak on a cold (minus 5 degrees) March morning in 1954, the above mentioned baker's dozen of adventurers and Bob LeBlanc, our cook, set out on a history-making jaunt to Phoenix. No more congenial or colorful group ever took to the back trails of Arizona trying to get away from it all. Though we knew what our destination looked like, few of us were acquainted with what adventure lay ahead between starting point and destination—that is, off the beaten path of railroads, highways and skyways. This trek, though it would not follow an exact "as the crow flies" course, would follow as short a route as would be feasible for horses to negotiate without undue discomfort to them or riders.

We would never be far from a road of some sort—maybe a paved highway but more likely a back country trail that one wouldn't want to put the family "limousine" on. A pickup would be more suited to the purpose. This trail must follow the horseback route close enough to permit a periodic liaison between the truck bearing the liquid refreshment and the riders. You can't successfully carry beer in a saddlebag; a trotting horse would have the stuff so shaken up you couldn't open a can or bottle without getting a shower of foam—"it's better to drink it than wear it," seemed to be a fitting motto to meet the situation.

The pickup would have to serve as a combination packhorse and refreshment stand with which to furnish the riders with the necessary remedy for the relief of sore muscles, blisters and other trail hazards. If your muscles are not sore, use some other excuse. On looking back, it took a lot of cure-all elixir to keep forward momentum on an even keel.

The cook truck was always a popular place to hang around.

Getting the refreshments delivered to the riders and finding a suitable trail would not be as difficult a task as it may sound. Paul Tissaw, the trail-boss, had mapped the trail in his mind in advance and knew where fences and other pitfalls might be encountered; in his cow-punching days he knew every nook and cranny in much of the area we would cover.

Many of the innovations we enjoyed on later trips were lacking on the first trip. Though inconvenient at the time, our impressions of that pioneering venture left lasting memories on all who experienced the adventure.

Diz's pickup truck was the cook wagon and all around "packhorse." Not only did this vehicle haul Dutch ovens and all the other cooking paraphernalia and utensils but our food supply, a small amount of horse feed, bed rolls—everything. A regular chuck wagon box had been built to set in the back end of the pickup; Diz had hinged the lid so it came down to form a work table for the cook. Add to this equipment the supply of beer and other refreshments (someone even slipped some soda pop in there) and that pickup was packed to the gills. Much of the bulkier horse feed, hay and grain, had been previously stashed along the route in strategic places where we could get at it each day, or as needed.

At noon stops we had to unload bedrolls, etc., to get at the horse feed and our own food; then reload again after we were through. We learned a lot on that pilot trip. The second trip and thereafter we had several vehicles to haul our equipment.

For a while before the journey started there was an anxious, sometimes frantic, search for horses. Most of us didn't own horses; we had to borrow them. We would have to refrain from following in the footsteps of the mountain men of old, who might have stolen them. Times have changed. As most of the horses we managed to get for the trip had been out on range forage, they had to be gathered and grained for a few days and shod to ready them for the trail ride.

"I don't want some crow-bait on this trip that can't hold up," was the trail boss' assessment of the situation.

I remember scrounging around in quest of a mount. My old friend, E. Ellis "Lucky" Starr, came to the rescue. He knew a fellow out at Cucamonga Junction who had a mule I could borrow. A mule? So what? Old Bill Williams himself often rode a mule in preference to a horse—more reliable, he claimed.

That's how I became acquainted with Chigger, a sure-footed little black mule. Later, at our first night's camp at Perkinsville, I learned about Chigger's past life. Nick Perkins owned and operated the Bar Cross, which included where we were camped for the night. Anyway, Nick recognized Chigger.

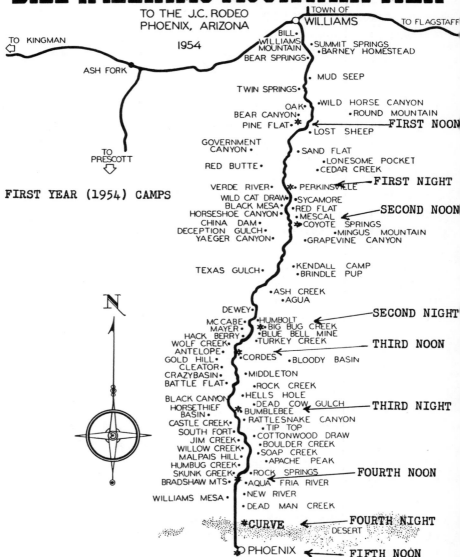

SOUTH ROUTE
OF THE
BILL WILLIAMS MOUNTAIN MEN
TO THE J.C. RODEO
PHOENIX, ARIZONA
1954

TO GRAND CANYON

TOWN OF
WILLIAMS

TO FLAGSTAFF

TO KINGMAN

BILL
WILLIAMS
MOUNTAIN
BEAR SPRINGS•

•SUMMIT SPRINGS
•BARNEY HOMESTEAD

ASH FORK

• MUD SEEP

TO PRESCOTT

TWIN SPRINGS•

OAK•
BEAR CANYON•
PINE FLAT•✱

•WILD HORSE CANYON
•ROUND MOUNTAIN
←— FIRST NOON

•LOST SHEEP

GOVERNMENT
CANYON •

•SAND FLAT
•LONESOME POCKET
•CEDAR CREEK

RED BUTTE •

FIRST YEAR (1954) CAMPS

VERDE RIVER•✱•PERKINSVILLE ←— FIRST NIGHT
WILD CAT DRAW• •SYCAMORE
BLACK MESA• •RED FLAT ←— SECOND NOON
HORSESHOE CANYON• •MESCAL
CHINA DAM• ✱COYOTE SPRINGS
DECEPTION GULCH• •MINGUS MOUNTAIN
YAEGER CANYON• •GRAPEVINE CANYON

TEXAS GULCH•
•KENDALL CAMP
•BRINDLE PUP

•ASH CREEK
•AGUA

N

DEWEY•
MC CABE• •HUMBOLT ←— SECOND NIGHT
MAYER• ✱BIG BUG CREEK
HACK BERRY• •BLUE BELL MINE
WOLF CREEK• •TURKEY CREEK ←— THIRD NOON
ANTELOPE•
GOLD HILL• ✱CORDES •BLOODY BASIN
CLEATOR•
CRAZYBASIN• •MIDDLETON
BATTLE FLAT•
•ROCK CREEK
BLACK CANYON• •HELLS HOLE
HORSETHIEF• •DEAD COW GULCH ←— THIRD NIGHT
BASIN • ✱BUMBLEBEE
CASTLE CREEK• • RATTLESNAKE CANYON
SOUTH FORT• • TIP TOP
JIM CREEK• •COTTONWOOD DRAW
WILLOW CREEK• •BOULDER CREEK
MALPAIS HILL• •SOAP CREEK
HUMBUG CREEK• •APACHE PEAK
SKUNK CREEK• •ROCK SPRINGS ←— FOURTH NOON
BRADSHAW MTS• •AQUA FRIA RIVER
WILLIAMS MESA • •NEW RIVER
•DEAD MAN CREEK

✱CURVE ←— FOURTH NIGHT
DESERT

PHOENIX ←— FIFTH NOON

PRESCOTT COURIER, INC.

Seems like Nick had come into possession of the little mule in its younger days—"smart as a whip and top notch for working cows with," said Nick. "He was just too little. Sooner or later he would break down under hard work.

"He was," reminisced Nick, "a perfect pet for someone with kids or he would be just right to haul dudes around on, if they were within reasonable weight limits."

The upshot was that Nick sold Chigger to Fred Harvey, Inc., for use at the Grand Canyon hauling dudes around and in the canyon. Nick had hung the handle "Chigger" on the mule because of the size of the animal. "He was hardly bigger than a chigger (a bothersome insect that infects livestock)," said Nick.

Further sleuthing divulged that after several years of canyon service, Chigger was turned out to a life of leisure in the Fred Harvey pasture at Del Rio. Eventually, Chigger was bought by the rancher at Cucamonga Junction, from whom I borrowed him for the trip.

In later years, I borrowed a mare from Harry Meier to use on the trail. After a couple of years of that, I bought the mare, Peggy O'Neill, a registered quarter mare. Although mares are frowned upon for use in extended trips such as our rendezvous ride, Peggy usually behaved in a ladylike manner.

The cook could always use help. On the day prior to leaving on our first trip, I cooked five pounds of pinto beans at home in a big pressure cooker to take along. Any connoisseur of pinto bean cookery will tell you that's no way to get the full flavor from that particular legume, but I didn't have time and we didn't have time on the trip to properly cook them in a Dutch oven. Anyway, we ate almost half of those beans at noon the first day, and that's a lot of beans!

As previously mentioned, Doc Stewart kept in touch by short wave radio. Verne Carothers informed him of the amount of beans being consumed, to which Doc quipped, "I hope to get good reports from the beans on our next transmission." Now, now, Doc! We missed Doc's droll Boston humor on the trip.

Our stops (noon and night) were never lengthy enough to cook stick-to-your-ribs beans and that is, or should be, a staple item of the diet on trail rides. To cook beans (pinto, that is . . . is there any other kind?) takes time. First, you have to pick the rocks out. No matter how many times they've been cleaned and re-cleaned, that one overlooked rock can raise hell with someone's bridgework and, out on the trail, you can be a long way from your dentist. Next, the beans have to be soaked for a few hours, preferably overnight. At lower altitudes like Phoenix (1,100 feet), the soaking is not necessary, but this trip starts at almost 7,000 feet elevation.

Being continually on the go, we didn't have time to devote to cow or sheep-camp cookery; that is, cooking in Dutch ovens buried in the ground. That requires lots of time to get the coals ready to cover the bottom, sides and top of the oven, and at the same time, to get the hole pre-heated, and then, to bury the food-laden ovens in the coals and dirt for ten or twelve hours. That would take too much time that we didn't have.

By making the "beer run" to keep up the morale of the riders, the pickup would, of necessity, be in use much of the time. The anesthetic quality of the brew, or stronger stuff, eased the pain of trail hazards—such as soothing muscles unused for years prior to the trip's start. All of this, of course, meant that there were times, especially at noon, when a meal had to be prepared in a hurry.

Any way you looked at it the cook would be working under difficult circumstances. He needed all the help we could give him not only on this first but subsequent trips as well. Although we might strive to act like the old time mountain men, our diet would be somewhat different from the beaver tails, buffalo humps and raw deer liver they lived on and seemingly enjoyed.

I scalped and sliced for frying enough potatoes to at least place or show in the *Guinness Book of Records.* I also washed enough dishes, pots and pans to have qualified for top honors in the Pearldiver-of-the-Month-Club by the time we reached Phoenix. It's sometimes hard to understand why so many pots and pans, *et al,* are used in preparing a meal, but they are used and they all have to be washed and stowed away three times a day. It all goes with the trip.

On the eve of the first rendezvous ride we had a parade

through Williams, starting at the east end of Bill Williams Avenue and ending at the hospital, at the other end of town, to give the patients therein a look at us. We were proud of our organization and anxious to show off our trappings and were agreeably surprised with the reception we received, with one noticeable exception. One motel owner sneered as we passed his motel and spouted to all within hearing distance—"just how corny can a bunch of grown men get?"

Regardless of that incident, locals and tourists alike produced cameras and the shutters clicked. Applause along the route also told us that we were on our way to being accepted by the public.

Later that year some of our newly-found friends among the Phoenix J.C.s happened to visit Williams. It also just happened that these people stayed at that particular motel. Seems like that motel owner could hardly contain himself until he joined up with that "corny" bunch of bums after learning from the Phoenix visitors that the Bill Williams Mountain Men were here to stay. That pre-rendezvous parade through Williams became a habit for many years afterward.

There was another sour note on the morning of the first day. As the group was leaving town, a bystander said (we were told later) "...they remind me of a bunch of politicians—they don't know where they are going; when they get there—if they do—they won't know where they are. The main difference is—these guys are spending their own money—the politicians gouge the taxpayers."

First the motel operator and then this clown. It would take a lot more than that to dampen our spirits. The Bill Williams Mountain Men were on their way to rendezvous!

That first day's ride of the initial trek was just getting nicely underway when an unexpected accident happened. The horses were approaching the old Barney homestead, eight miles out, when something spooked Ray Stewart's horse. The animal promptly unloaded Ray into a pile of boulders. Fortunately, what might have been a serious accident didn't materialize into more than a broken finger, the ring finger on his left hand.

It happened that some of the wives drove out along the road

We had a roof over us as the cook crew went to work at Perkinsville.

we were following to see how their spouses were holding up. This circumstance afforded Ray a ride back to town for medical care. His horse was driven along empty with the group and Ray met us further along the route to finish the ride.

That morning Rod had tied his bedroll on a packhorse. "That's the way the old-timers did it," he explained. "See that diamond-hitch?" he gestured, "that's the way the old packers secured a pack."

He led the packhorse a few miles; then, as the horse seemed not to mind the burden and was following nicely with the loose horses, the halter rope was taken off. All went well for several miles.

Near Summit Springs, about twelve miles out, that packhorse had a change-of-mind about the pack. He bucked a time or two and then took off across country, headed east. While the others continued on the journey, Rod and Paul took the trail of the errant packhorse. That chase covered some three miles through the brush and rocks, finally ending near the top of Frog Hill, on the Whitehorse Lake road. They and the packhorse caught up with the group at noon camp on Pine Flat. Rod's bedroll was there added to the rest of the bedrolls on the pickup. From then on, the pack animals only hauled packs in the parade later on in Phoenix.

From the noon stop at Pine Flat, the trail followed the old Perkinsville road down past Bear Canyon, then on past the Golden Buckskin and Yellowjacket flagstone quarries, in addition to other, mostly nameless workings, to the Drake road and then on to Perkinsville.

South Road (Williams-Perkinsville Highway) found a better alignment after our first rendezvous trip and after several more rendezvous trips via Pine Flat and the quarries, we were more or less forced to follow the new road. We always thought that the old road was more picturesque, but it had been abandoned and subsequent storms had washed it out to where it was impassable to vehicular travel. In that rough canyon country, there was no possibility of circumventing these washouts. The beer truck would be completely unable to reach the riders and these

"Tea" party at Perkinsville

characters would never tolerate the threat of dehydration for the several hours it would take to reach them via the long detour ahead.

That first night we camped at Perkinsville, on the Verde. Nick Perkins had lots of corrals we could use. We put our bedrolls on the sand near the bridge—some of us under the bridge (what a mistake that was you'll see a little later). By the time supper was ready Nick and Ben, one of his sons, had joined us.

After supper Ben went home and brought back his guitar. From then until about two-thirty or three o'clock the next morning there was no sleep for anyone within hearing distance. In the early night hours, Ben got in his car. I believe Rod went with him, and went to Jerome, about twenty miles away, to get a new supply of corn squeezin's. Before they left and after getting back he roared back and forth across the bridge a couple of times to entertain us with the thunderous clatter the car made on the loose planks of the bridge.

Some of us gave up and sought our bedrolls long before Ben and a few of the more hardy mountain men ran out of booze and breath with which to indulge in what they hoped passed for singing around the campfire. As a choral group the chances were extremely slim that they would ever make the big time.

They might be classified as—"not much for pretty but hell for stout."

I think I was about to doze off in merciful sleep when Ben decided to go home. Nick had long since given up and gone home. Ben's farewell consisted of four or five more noisy trips back and forth across the rattling plants of the bridge, at the same time yelling—"time to get up—do you want to sleep all of your lives—etc." Loose sand and rocks, dropped on the planks by previous truck traffic, showered on those of us who had our beds under the bridge.

Thus dropped the curtain on a long-to-be-remembered day and most of the night. Two hours later it was time to feed the horses and get ready for another day's activities.

That morning was a time for second thoughts for those whose time spent in the saddle before the ride started had been minimal or non-existent. Some few, who never dreamed a horse could do that to them, groaned to themselves and winced as they eased their tender buttocks gingerly into the saddle for another day on the hurricane deck of Old Smokey.

They tightened their determination another notch, took a good-sized belt from the bottle going the rounds (something heretofore unheard of this early in the day) and urged their horses forward—ever so gently, please.

"If it's any consolation," suggested some kind-hearted soul—"our predecessors often underwent privations far worse—"

Comforting words. By the end of the trip they'd have callouses on top of callouses, and the discomfort would be lost in memory. This day's ride would be shorter, for which some were thankful.

It's surprising the number of objects that can be forgotten by a person when packing for a trip. At breakfast that morning at Perkinsville the absence of these forgotten items started to be felt. It was—"Hey, Spike, will you be anywhere near civilization today? If you are, pick up a face towel for me—I had to use my shirt tail this morning—not that I care what Emily Post might say to that, but a towel would be better—"

Another one—"You can run your fingers through your hair

and get by without a comb by putting your hat on, but how the hell can you brush your teeth without a brush? Will you get me a tooth brush and some tooth paste? I could use a comb, too."

This was only the second day out. As the trip continued there were daily side trips to "civilization" to replenish various needs that had been overlooked or lost. As carefully as the cook wagon supplies are put together, there's always something lacking that has to be taken care of. This calls for a three-way liaison among "civilization," cook and riders. The desired objective is to maintain a camp life considerably above the level of abject poverty but not quite like swinging it at the Waldorf Astoria. We were getting away from the pampering of home life but not to the point of being uncomfortable—we hoped.

Face towels, after use in the morning, were sometimes too wet to put in the duffel bags. In that case they were tied on the truck some place to dry. Our truck usually looked like a re-run of The Grapes of Wrath family leaving the dust bowl states. It took only a short time for the towels to dry in the breeze. They were then folded and put in the truck cab. Hopefully, everybody got his own towel back.

Leaving Perkinsville, the trail led along the road toward Jerome. Part way up the side of Mingus Mountain the road joined the old abandoned narrow-gauge railroad alignment that extended from Jerome to its mainline terminal with the Peavine (A.T. & S.F.) railroad, near Prescott. Paul Tissaw, trail boss, led the riders along the narrow-gauge alignment, then a well-traveled road, about two miles toward Prescott where they came to a side road. We then took off on this new road, through a gate. After following that road (in places primitive) for about two miles, we reached Coyote Springs Ranch, where we had set up for the noon stop.

Coyote Springs was out in the middle of Lonesome Valley, below the western slope of Mingus Mountain.

After leaving Coyote Springs Ranch, the riders soon reached Alternate Highway 89 that meanders from Prescott over Mingus to Jerome and from there to where it eventually joins Highway 89 in Flagstaff. They were forced to follow Alternate 89 about two miles toward Jerome, to the Dewey cutoff road, and then south again on the Dewey road. This detour was due to the fence paralleling the highway not having a gate in that area—annoying, but one of those things we had to expect and endure.

Our trail led down the Dewey cutoff road across the lower end of Lonesome Valley, through Dewey and Humboldt. By then, fatigue from lack of sleep the night before had begun to catch up. Even those more or less used to roughing it began to droop.

Camp for the night was set up at Goat Ranch, a couple of miles below Humboldt. Where that name "Goat Ranch" came from, I don't know—they were running cattle when we were there. Close by, on Highway 69, construction had just started on a cafe, later named Reata Pass.

Being that close to a well-traveled highway, we attracted a lot of visitors and that (again) cut in on our getting a good night's rest. Aw, well, maybe the next night we would catch up on some much-needed sleep.

Leaving Goat Ranch, our trail closely followed the highway (69) south as far as Mayer. From there, we took the route of the old highway (Black Canyon) south.

The course of Big Bug Creek meandered aimlessly in the general direction we were headed. We crossed it three or four times in the next few miles. We also crossed such interestingly-named geographic entities as: Turkey Creek, Wolf Creek, and I think there was a Coyote Gulch along there somewhere.

We nooned at Cordes, about three or four miles west of the present Cordes Junction. From there, we followed the old Black Canyon Highway down into Black Canyon and on to Bumblebee.

We camped about a half mile below Bumblebee that night. Through the years, a large sandy flat had been formed by the meandering, then dry, Bumblebee Creek. When heavy storms hit on the watershed, sometimes miles away, this ordinarily mild-mannered creek had at times become a raging torrent which deposited a sandy floor along and near the creekbed.

We picked up a plentiful supply of driftwood which had been

deposited nearby by past storms for fuel. An ideal camp. Nearby cottonwood trees made natural posts for use in building a rope corral for the horses. Downstream a short distance was a natural pool of water left from the last rainstorm. We filled all containers for camp use before the horses got there.

All of the riders got into camp early that afternoon. The horses were taken care of and there was little to do except indulge in a little imbibing until suppertime. That elbow bending exercise was a daily ritual which helped one forget the bruises and other hardships encountered during the day.

A ranch house and outbuildings were screened from our view by a row of cottonwoods. Closer by was a pond of water where a "dozer" had scooped a large hole in the sand. The day was somewhere above the 80-degree mark which was uncomfortably warm away from the shade of the trees—especially for this bunch of mountain dwellers.

Rod, closely followed by several others, started for the inviting pool, shedding clothes as they went. A swim would be cooling and invigorating before supper.

That's when the rancher, who until then hadn't been any-where in sight, put in an appearance from behind the trees. The "swimmin' hole" was definitely off limits, he said, due to its being his source of water for domestic use. His tone of voice and gestures indicated that he meant there would be no swimming there that day.

There is a time when even a general can retire from the battlefield wihout losing too much face when confronted by overwhelming odds. Though the odds did not seem great, our "troops" decided that this was the time for such a discreet maneuver as retreating hastily from the scene. They gathered up their clothes (one or two men were in the buff already) and hastily conceded the skirmish to the rancher. You know—when in Rome, do as the Romans, but don't swim in their drinking water.

The evening cooled off comfortably and by the time darkness descended, a calm settled over the camp. Before long a full moon arose, clearing the sharply-defined mountain range on the

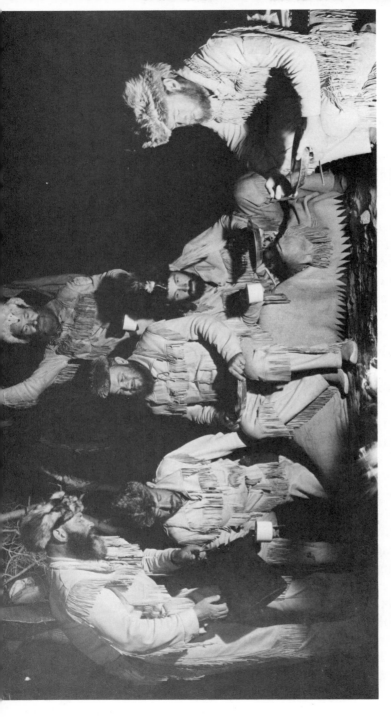

Hurley Wright pours (I'm sure it's coffee) as (l. to r.) Louis Landry, Fred Theroux, "Spike" Way, Oscar Skaggs and John Girvin look on.

east side of the canyon.

One could feel the desert coming to life, as the wildlife, that had been semi-dormant through the heat of the day, started out in search of food in the cool of the evening. The eerie bark of a marauding coyote off in the distance was answered by a yelp closer by—testing their communications system. That would go on most of the night or until their hunger was sated, but it wouldn't bother us. There had been very little sleep on the two previous nights on the trail. We'd make up for that tonight.

Soon the only noise to disturb the quiet night was the mostly-subdued snores of the men, occasionally punctuated by the distant haunting bark of a coyote on the prowl—nature's own symphony of the great outdoors.

It cooled off early the next morning, a typical desert morning in the early spring, provoking a remark that something might have crawled in our beds with us to get out of the cold.

"Which reminds me of a story a fellow told me one time," said Jake. Everybody close by listened attentively, as Jake was never given to excess conversation.

Seems like Jake's friend was a cowboy back in Texas. He, the friend, was working a roundup. On awakening one morning he found that a rattlesnake had coiled up on his bedroll to absorb the heat from the bed.

"He got out of that bed awful careful," mused Jake, as he shook out his boots before putting them on.

Being early in March it was too early for buzztails to be out and around, but I noticed that I was not the only one who gave my blankets an extra shaking out before rolling them up that morning.

Things were going smoothly on the fourth day. It was early in the afternoon. The riders were strung out a half mile or more near Skunk Creek. Bill Lilly decided to give his horse a rest. He unsaddled his horse, threw the saddle and bridle on the pickup and caught Chigger, the little black mule from the string of extras in the remuda. He wouldn't need a saddle or bridle as that mule wasn't about to stray away from his equine friends on the trail.

Bill settled himself on Chigger with a can of beer in hand and started out. He hadn't given much thought to the practical jokers among the group, which was a mistake—a big mistake. Two of those characters, Paul and Jake, came up behind the unsuspecting bareback rider, one on each side. They each held the end of a rope which was stretched across behind the mule. Somehow they got the rope under the mule's tail and rasped it across a very tender part of the animal's anatomy.

Needless to say, Chigger wanted no part of that. He headed skyward and so did Bill. When the mule came down, he was several feet down the trail and moving on out. Bill, on his return to *terra firma*, was standing in a clump of brush and marveling at his good luck: he still had the can of beer in his hand; he hadn't spilled a drop of it; and, he had landed in a non-prickly bush. Considering the fact that that part of Arizona is covered with many varieties of cactus and other desert flora—all profuse with sticky spines—Bill was lucky, indeed!

We were lucky, too. Bill was a chef at Rod's Steak House back home. He put in much time on that and subsequent trips around the cook fire, helping the cook. We sure didn't want him to get laid up. A lot of steaks required his expert attention.

Originally, the fourth (and last) night's campsite was intended to be a dry camp (we'd have to haul water) about two miles up the highway from the Curve. The Curve was sixteen miles north of Phoenix, where I-17 makes its last curve before a straight shot into Phoenix.

Bob (the cook) and I explored the area near the Curve in the beer truck. The Curve was a restaurant with a beer license and appeared to be a very nice oasis in the desert. The owners, Dee and Joe, went all out to be accommodating: unlimited camping space for us and the horses to sack out; water—lots of it; and, wash tubs to water our horses. Why pass up Utopia?

We went back up the trail, contacted the trail boss and explained the situation to him. He said to go ahead and set up camp at the Curve. That set a precedent. From then on, the last night's camp was always at the Curve. Dee and Joe treated us royally and always had the latch-string out for us at their place.

The Curve was a home away from home. Dee lived in a large

housetrailer behind the restaurant. Included in our deluxe treatment was the use of her bath tub. Wow! After four days collection of sweat and trail dust, we luxuriated in a warm bath—scrumptious! Don't spread this around, but some of us even used some perfumed bubble bath stuff that Dee gave us. The mountain men of old would roll over in their graves if they knew that we had replaced beaver musk with bubble bath.

We had been close to that much water only once on the trail. That was at Perkinsville where the Verde flowed past. We could, of course, have bathed in that frigid water; but in March, the temperature of the water and weather tends to discourage a closer acquaintance with the stuff than an occasional drink of same—we made coffee with it, too! Being the first day out, we hadn't yet collected enough dirt to worry about. For washing our hands and faces, we took the time to heat water on the fire.

Dee ran an ad in a Phoenix paper after the first year announcing the Mountain Men's arrival on a certain date. A lot of people came out to see us, some of them, year after year. Kids of all ages swarmed over our camp to see and talk to the "men of the mountains" and have a short ride on their horses, the latter under strict supervision, of course. After all, those horses had been on the trail all day and wanted the saddles off so they could roll the itch off. We used a couple of wash tubs to water them.

The weather was ideal during the entire trip. When leaving Williams the first morning, the mercury hovered around zero and a little below, necessitating the wearing of jackets until late morning. The sun was out bright and, with the drop in altitude, the day became warmer as we went along. The second morning leaving Perkinsville it was cold along the Verde River and on the trail for little more than an hour. From there on until the last morning, leaving the Curve, the weather was on the warm-to-hot side.

The Curve, as we knew it, is no longer there. The buildings have long since been razed to make room for something else. Progress?

That last half day a light drizzle of rain plagued the riders, but spirits were high (in more ways than one) when our pilgrimage finally reached the fairgrounds in Phoenix around noon. We

Bill Williams Mountain Men beam with success after first historical ride to Phoenix on March 17, 1954 (back row, l. to r.) Bob LeBlanc (cook), Paul Tissaw, Jake January and Rod Graves; (center row) E. J. Theroux, Sr., Ray Stewart, Fred Theroux, John Mills, Bill Lilly, Thurman Mayes, Louis Landry and Denton "Diz" Dean; (front row) Verne Carothers and Thomas E. "Spike" Way.

didn't feel too bad when we learned they were getting a snowstorm at home—rain is much easier to shovel.

Rod, Paul and Diz had made a reconnaissance trip by car to Phoenix a few days before the ride started to meet with the J.C.s to warn them we were coming. They (the J.C.s) arranged for stall space at the fairgrounds—plenty of enclosed stalls (such pampering our horses never had before) and two large tack rooms. In general, they rolled out the red carpet of welcome when we got there on the cold (for Phoenix) rainy noon of March 17, 1954.

The initial rendezvous trip was by far the most adventurous of our jaunts—the challenge of the unknown. How will we be treated and accepted by people along the route? After we reached our destination? What's around the next bend in the trail? Over the next hill? How far out of the way will we find a gate in that drift fence off in the distance? Will we find available water, or how far will we have to haul it?

A lot of questions, and some that had not yet been asked, were answered on the first trip—more on succeeding trips. Somehow the later rendezvous trips, although unforgettable and enjoyable adventures, did not have the impressionable impact we experienced on *Numero Uno*.

One of the brightest of Phoenix's night spots in 1954 was the Westward Ho's Concho Room. What better place for a bunch of country boys to seek entertainment while rendezvousing in Phoenix?

The marquee on the Westward Ho proclaimed the King Sisters and Alvino Rey to be the stellar attractions in the Concho Room at the time. Alvino Rey was married to one of the King Sisters. Several of us paid them a visit.

This was before the advent of the hippie element who threw away their razors and infested society like a horde of locusts. Consequently, our facial foliage was more or less a novelty and we got along great with the entertainers. Between their song numbers, the King Sisters sat with us and visited and before the evening was over we were good friends.

Two nights later we again invaded the Concho Room, taking along some of the others who had missed out the first night. We were greeted with—"Where were you guys last night? We missed you. There was a group of revelers who came in and wanted to know—'where are those guys with the whiskers and buckskins from the mountains?' "

A-h-h-h-h, such is fame—fleeting and unexpected!

The Westward Ho, once a leading downtown hotel, has since been reconstructed into an apartment building and the glamor of the Concho Room is long gone. What used to be one of the livelier night spots has long since joined the limbo of cherished memories: the Corinthian Room, downstairs in the old Adams—the Adams, itself—Joe Gaddis's Silver Spur—all are gone. These and others have vanished in the name of progress since the first year of our time-honored rendezvous trips; even the Guys and Dolls, way out on East Washington, joined the ranks of the has-beens—they did, however, open up again in later years under a different name.

The first two or three days of the rides were always the roughest. Very few of the members rode every day in their normal home life. They were not conditioned for the trip; consequently, nearly everyone rode high in the saddle at the start to give the blisters a chance to cool off, wondering all the time how anything stuffed with hay could be so hard to sit on. Old Panther or Old Busthead, taken internally of course, offered some balm for the comfort of the rider. By the end of the day the average rider felt little or no pain.

The mountain man of former days had to have all his faculties in peak condition at all times to survive in the wilderness. He couldn't afford to let some Indian creep up on him while on a trapping expedition. That meant no intoxicating liquor at any time except at rendezvous, where he made up for lost time.

In later years we had one guest rider who annually got roaring drunk the first day of the trip. Every year for several years he followed the same pattern—usually on the verge of passing out all the first day, then rarely taking a drink the rest of the entire trip. Once he had to be tied in his saddle, at his insistence, to keep from falling off; he insisted on riding all the way—and he did. From there on to night camp two other riders flanked him, one on either side, to see that no trouble befell him.

The most serious problem facing today's counterpart of the mountain man of old would probably be falling off his horse or another discomforting predicament (as reported by the press)— "one of the new riders stopped to visit with a tourist along the route on the second day out. In their conversation, the tourist said, of the rider's sunburned face, 'your face is sure red'—to which the rider answered—'you ought to see the other end.' "

Paul Tissaw rides in the Phoenix parade.

Washington, D.C.

Eastward Ho!

The Old Santa Fe Trail was scouted more than a century ago by the mountain men. On a cold January day in 1961 these same old rough and tough characters of the frontier would have rolled over in their graves if they could have seen inside one of the Santa Fe's sleek streamliners, the **Grand Canyon Limited,** eastbound, as it streaked through the mountains and across the plains—through the same rugged terrain where those hardy frontiersmen had been the forerunners of the later advance of colonization to the West. Inside that fast train was, of all things, a group of those same whiskered, intrepid mountain men of the western frontier.

Mountain men? Yes, as if from a capricious time warp that had suddenly regressed history to the Old West's most daring and romantic past, there had suddenly emerged a group almost as genuine in attire and appearance as Old Bill Williams or Jim (Gabe) Bridger. Modern railroad accommodations would be the temporary home of these seemingly reincarnated mountain men on their way to Washington, D.C., to ride as Arizona's official delegation in the presidential inaugural parade. Up ahead, safely ensconced in palatial streamlined horse cars, rode the hardy range horses of this group. These mustangs of Arizona never had it so good.

We had carried off top honors in the "Best Mounted Group" division in Phoenix's parade for seven years in a row and we did equally well in other parades elsewhere, including Tucson, Wickenburg, Tombstone, Scottsdale, Prescott, Flagstaff, Winslow; we even branched out in May 1959, and joined the ranks of Las Vegas, Nevada's Helldorado Days Parade. Our acceptance in all these places was overwhelming.

Our courage thus bolstered, we made an effort to break into the coveted ranks of the renowned Rose Bowl Parade in Pasadena, California. Needless to say, we were handed a polite, but firm—"NO." Seems like our horses, purposely uncurried

Getting ready for the Washington, D.C. trip by making a deposit at the bank in downtown Williams. Some tourists thought we had made a "gunpoint" withdrawal.

from a winter's life in the wilderness, to fit the character of our venture, would not fit into that parade of flowers and immaculately-groomed horseflesh. In other words—we didn't have the necessary "spit and polish" to be acceptable in the Parade Of The Roses.

Had we broken that barrier, we might have added not only color but aroma to the proceedings—especially to those downwind. But, alas—it was not our lot to grace the streets of Pasadena. But we wouldn't want or have it any other way; we had an act that, literally speaking, would lose much of its appeal if it was cleaned up (no pun intended).

Then came our chance at the "big time." Governor Paul Fannin appointed the Bill Williams Mountain Men as Arizona's official entry in the Presidential Inaugural Parade in Washington, D.C. That was why we were aboard the ***Grand Canyon Limited*** that day in mid-January, 1961. We were on our way to break into the coveted ranks of the grand daddy of all parades; perhaps we would pick up another trophy to add to our growing collection.

Before this trek to the nation's capital could become a reality, preparations were in order. Of foremost importance was the launching of a campaign to raise money—lots of money. The magnitude of the intended venture was enough to boggle the minds of this bunch of country boys—transportation for men and horses—feeding the same bunch—accommodations—on and on—

We dug in our toenails. We had raffles and we put on dances throughout Northern Arizona. We begged, borrowed, but stopped short of stealing. We wrote letters to businesses far and wide in Arizona who might donate to our cause. To get statewide backing we temporarily changed our name to the "Arizona Mountain Men."

For this letter-writing campaign we had special letterheads printed proclaiming: "ARIZONA MOUNTAIN MEN— PRESIDENTIAL INAUGURAL COMMITTEE—Rod Graves, chairman, and members Gordon McDowell and Thomas E. Way." In its entirety this was strictly for window dressing—an ad hoc arrangement to represent the entire state in the inaugural parade. When the Washington trip was completed we would (and did) revert to being the Bill Williams Mountain Men.

We had the wholehearted support of various organizations far and wide who helped us raise money. The Coconino County Sheriff's Posse was especially helpful to our cause.

After what seemed an interminable time, we had enough coin of the realm cornered and banked to finance the trip. Our dream was about to become a reality. Move over Washington—here we come!

The day of departure came at last. Our long months of preparation had finally borne fruit. It was time to load up and hit the trail.

When the horses were loaded in the baggage cars (converted to accommodate horses) along with Tuffy our mascot who, in his cage, would accompany the horses, we were getting close to the time to bid adieu to our families. Our tack, saddles, travois (two of them) and other parade paraphernalia, guns, etc., had already been loaded in the cars that had been spotted earlier that day at the old Santa Fe freight depot in Williams. Fred "Perico" Avila was busily painting "ARIZONA MOUNTAIN MEN" on the sides of the cars for the benefit of interested observers along the route who could see who would be whizzing past on the train.

Though we would temporarily be known as the "Arizona Mountain Men," Perico, in a place or two, carried away by the gaiety of the occasion, decided that we were still the "Bill Williams Mountain Men," and spread some of the paint accordingly.

TV crews from Phoenix were on hand to cover the loading of the horses. After all, this was an historic first in the seven year life of the organization.

As paymaster, I had to get to the bank before they closed the doors that day to get the necessary funds to cover the trip. Thirty-three members, guests and wranglers were each given $150 spending money for which they were required to sign so that I could keep an accurate account. In addition, the three wranglers were each paid $25 per diem.

The nose count of the first inaugural trip was:

M. E. Coffee	Pete Miller
Denton "Diz" Dean	Jerry Payne
Gene Doyle	Paul Tissaw
J. W. Duffield	Oscar Skaggs
Bill Evans	Bill Freeman
Ben Fillmore	Bill Sutton
Rod Graves	Fred Theroux
Louis Landry	A. H. "Rudy" Ruddock
Charlie Sharp	Thomas E. "Spike" Way
Martin C. "Doc" Flohr	Hurley Wright
Bill Lilly	C. T. Mullen (guest)
John Maillie	John Girvin (guest)
Thurman Mayes	Bill Nixon (press-guest)
Gordon McDowell	Archie Morris (AHP-guest)
George McNelly	Harvey Golightly (AHP-guest)

Wranglers—George Williams—Bob Dean—Louie Peters.

THE KEY TO THE CITY—Mayor Walter J. Guenther presents key to the city to Jerry Duffield (left), president of Arizona's famous Bill Williams Mountain Men who are en route to Washington, D. C., to participate Friday in the inaugural parade of President-elect John F. Kennedy. Presentation of the key was made when the 35-man Arizona organization stopped at the Santa Fe depot here Sunday. Other Mountain Men in the photo are Martin C. Flohr (left) and Rod Graves. The beards, incidentally are real.—Democrat Staff Photo.

★ ★ ★

Mountain Men | Radar Tower Collapses

Day Visit to | I. S.......... 28 M....

The *Arizona Republic* had generously allowed their correspondent, Bill Nixon, to accompany us. Bill not only got us good coverage in the news media but took a lot of good pictures of and for us, covering the entire adventure. He even broke his leg in line of duty (as described later).

Later that afternoon the horse cars were shunted to Winslow where they were serviced to supply water for the stock, washrooms, etc., for the trek. Our chair car was placed on a siding at Williams Junction where we boarded late that night after the Williams bars closed; perish the thought that we should embark on this all-important journey in a dehydrated condition. After all, we had heard vague rumors that our train would cross Kansas, a state in which John Barleycorn was known to be frowned upon in certain circles—we would take no chances!

The *Grand Canyon Limited,* a top-line Santa Fe passenger train, picked up our car about two o'clock the next morning and took us to Winslow where our horse cars were added to the *Limited's* string and we were on our way to visit the new president.

Late afternoon of the same day, our train wound its way eastward through Raton Pass, past the grave of Dick Wootton, a mountain man buddy of Bill Williams. They both knew this area well. Old Bill met his fate, in 1849, less than a hundred miles northeast of Wootton's final resting place.

About six o'clock the next morning, somewhere in Kansas, a porter came through the door on the end of our car. He had a steaming coffee pot and a lot of paper cups. What a great way to wake up—believe me that coffee hit the spot!

"The coffee's on Rudy," the porter explained. He also told us that Rudy Ruddock had ordered and paid for the coffee earlier that morning (we didn't get to sleep till the wee hours). I never knew of a time when Rudy wasn't doing something nice for someone else; it was a way of life for him.

When the train reached Fort Madison, Iowa, the Chamber of Commerce of that city arranged to have the Santa Fe hold the train long enough for a friendly get-together. Those people know how to throw a party. The mayor presented us with the key to the city and gave us each a bottle of wine from a winery across the Mississippi River in nearby Nauvoo, Illinois.

Next stop—Chicago, where two TV crews and the press met us at Dearborn Station. It was about seven o'clock p.m. and the early darkness of the January night was dissipated by a bank of lights along the platform. Thora and Merle Cowan, former Williams residents, were on hand for a visit. A crowd gathered around us, wanting to see our mascot, Tuffy the lion cub. Tuffy obliged by clawing his cage and airing his teeth for the people when he was exposed to the bright lights. Louie Landry got too close to the cage and Tuffy sank a claw into his hand, a painful reminder to keep a safe distance from the excitable cat.

We were also met in Chicago by Chuck McKenna, vice-president of Zellerbach Paper Products. Chuck had been a guest on a couple of our rendezvous trips. While our cars were being switched from Santa Fe to the Pennsylvania line for the balance of the trip Chuck took over our welfare. We had about three hours layover while our cars were switched over so we could continue on to Washington.

Chuck took us to Diamond's and wined and dined us in regal fashion. He introduced us as "some damn nice guys to ride the trail with."

The steaks at Diamond's were as good as Rod's steaks back home—and that's saying a lot. The liquor bill alone was $268— but, as Chuck said—"none of you are driving, so drink up—just imagine you're back on the trail from Williams to Phoenix."

When we came out of Diamond's, about six of us climbed into a taxi in front of the place and told the driver—"take us to the closest night club."

He started the engine and drove across the intersection and stopped, after a total journey of about 100 feet. "Here you are," he said.

The rest of the bunch walked over from Diamond's without too much effort or discomfort. Us country boys are just going to have to get used to life in the city or stay back in the boondocks.

At a brief stop in Pittsburgh, Pennsylvania, I visited with my brother-in-law Sam and his daughter Jill who had come down to the depot to see me. Jill was quite impressed with Tuffy and the horses that could be seen from the open doors. It was in Pittsburgh that Bob Dean added a little humor to the situation. The water pressure system on these cars operates by a pump powered by belt and pully from the wheels' axles. When the car stops, the pressure pump does likewise.

Bob came out of the washroom with the statement—"I was only about half washed when the spring went dry!"

On our arrival in Washington late in the afternoon we were bivouacked at the Pentagon Motel in Arlington, Virginia, close to the Pentagon Building. The horses were trucked out to the Rock Creek Stables, also in Virginia, where they had a good roll on *terra firma* for the first time since they left home several days previously.

Five Arizona mountain men perch on a fence at the Rock Creek Stables with their horses in the background. Paul Tissaw, Martin C. Flohr, Pete Miller, Spike Way and C. T. Mullen are here for the Inaugural Parade Friday. (Story on Page B-1.)—Star Staff Photo by Francis Routt.

The next two days we took in Washington and environs. Most of us took a bus tour across two or three state boundaries. Several states are bundled together in a small space around there. We went to Mount Vernon, George Washington's old estate, and other historical points of interest. In Washington itself, Ford's Theater (where Lincoln was shot) was undergoing extensive repairs and renovation and had been for several years and would not be completed in the foreseeable future; all of this due to "typical Washington thinking." That was a hackneyed phrase which we would repeatedly be exposed to during our sojourn in the nation's capital. The Ford's Theater repairs were reportedly being done with monies received from public subscription. Some of the fellows visited the Peterson House (where Lincoln died), across the street from Ford's Theater.

We visited the Department of Justice building where we shook hands with J. Edgar Hoover, top man of the Department of Justice, and had our picture taken with him. They took us on a tour through the building. Down at the shooting range in the basement we watched experts demonstrate handgun shooting. The accuracy of those guys is almost unbelievable.

One day, some of us were invited to, and did join members of the National Press Club for lunch. We also witnessed the colorful changing-of-the-guard ritual at the Tomb of the Unknown Soldier in Arlington National Cemetery.

We went back out to the Rock Creek Stables to visit our horses. They never had it so good: our western mustangs were used to living in the open without the comfort of an enclosed stable and a roof over their heads when it stormed. Here, they were living in clover with all the trimmings.

The *Washington* (DC) *Evening Star* had a picture of five of us perched on a fence at the stables in their January 18, 1961, issue. The *National Geographic* magazine had a cut-down version of the same picture in their April 1961, issue.

The Smithsonian Institution was another place we visited and enjoyed. It would take a month to see everything there. On our limited time schedule we, like our horses, were living it up on a limited scale.

Toward evening on the day before the parade, a snow storm

F.B.I. director J. Edgar Hoover met with representatives of the Arizona Mountain Men on January 18, 1961. Pictured with Mr. Hoover (l. to r.) are: John Girvin, Rudy Ruddock, Gene Doyle, Ben Fillmore, John Maillie, Fred Theroux, Bill Freeman, Denton Dean, Everett Coffee, Bill Sutton, Oscar Skaggs, Mr. Hoover, Pete Miller, Louis Landry, Thomas E. Way, Gordon McDowell, Arizona Highway patrolman Harvey Golightly, Bill Evans, Arizona Highway patrolman Archie Morris and Bill Nixon of the **Arizona Republic**.

descended on Washington. Later that night most of us were in the crowded downtown hotel lobbies handing out pamphlets extolling the wonders of Arizona. We had been furnished with several thousand booklets containing writeups of interesting places to visit in each of Arizona's counties including, of course, our own Grand Canyon.

C. T. Mullen (one of our guests), Everett Coffee, and I found ourselves in a booth in a bar of a large hotel. Sitting with us was a reporter who claimed to have an "in" with the president-elect and family. He could, he confided, arrange for one of us to dance with Jackie Kennedy at the inaugural ball the next night. This benefactor knew one of Jackie's hair dressers or ladies-in-waiting, or someone close to the first-lady-to-be, who would make the necessary arrangements. The main drawback to that arrangement was that nobody knew which ball the Kennedys would attend and at what time—the inaugural ball was to be held simultaneously in seven locations and the presidential party was to put in a brief appearance at all of them at some, as yet unknown, time that night.

Our newly-found confidante might be just another Washington misplaced big-shot with a good line of malarkey—Washington is full of them. This one, however, was later pointed out to us as Earl Wilson, a Washington columnist who did indeed know his way around the big town. The "dance with Jackie" routine didn't materialize (well, now—after all—what did you expect?). We didn't see "Earl Wilson" again.

The hotel lobby was filled to capacity. There wasn't even standing room left. Some of the people probably came in out of the blowing snow seeking refuge from the storm which was then nearing blizzard proportions. Suddenly someone near a front door shrieked and the nearby crowd took up the chant—"Sinatra!!" Sure enough a battering-ram formation of brawny musclemen bored through the crowd to a bank of elevators. "Old Blue Eyes" was surrounded by a bevy of beautiful ladies-in-waiting. They were all in a bunch and were surrounded by an outer circle of bodyguards, who looked like they might be on loan from the Washington Redskins football team.

It's cocktail time with Paul and Leo at a Washington, D.C. gathering.

A little later another group, including some of the Kennedy clan and similarly guarded, came in, passing through the lobby to the elevators where they were whisked away from the crowd to the safety of the upper floors. They were also accompanied by a covey of female attendants and bodyguards. Scuttlebutt had it that Sinatra and the Kennedys had two of the upper floors reserved.

When the storm hadn't let up by late that night, we started looking for transportation back to our motel. Taxis were at a premium; they seemed to be operated only in the downtown area. In a snowstorm Washingtonians are helpless (at least from our observation). In two inches of snow on the streets people lose all sense of responsibility. They leave their cars and start out walking—some cars are deserted in the middle of the street. Even taxi drivers become befuddled and refuse to get out in the storm. I know I've driven in much worse weather in and around Williams without worry or hesitation.

In Washington, taxis are operated by anyone over twenty-one years of age who has an operable vehicle, a driver's license and the necessary liability insurance to cover the operation. That's free trade wherein no taxi company can corner the market. Surely, we thought there must be a cab somewhere. Finally, one came along with a lady driver. She was a little braver than the rest; she was also talkative. She had—"three school-age children to raise and a sick husband."

Without too much belief in her tale of woe (cabbies always have a good line) we headed out for the Pentagon Motel. The lady didn't seem too scared of the snow, so we reached our destination, after having passed untold numbers of deserted "snowbound" cars along the way. We made a generous donation toward the upkeep of our driver's disadvantaged family.

Another cab stopped at another downtown hotel and several mountain men surged around it. The driver tried to explain that he wasn't about to go "dat far," and "acrost dat bridge in dat snowstorm." Our motel was across the Potomac and in a different town, Arlington, Virginia, from downtown Washington. The conversation had just about reached an impasse. Hurley Wright disgustedly asked the driver—"if we can find another driver, can he use your cab?"

That cabbie took an in-depth look at Hurley, who towered over him like Goliath over David. He shuddered and finally nodded assent.

"Move over—the driver's here—!" exploded Hurley, as he gave the guy a shove across the seat and moved in under the steering wheel. "Just point out the way to go."

The trip was completed without further complications. At the motel, the riders took up a collection and gave it to the cabbie along with a pat on the back. As he drove away mumbling unintelligibly to himself he didn't even look back. As Hurley watched the disappearing taxi, he said—"I hated to turn that boy loose on his own—I don't think he can find his way back home by himself." (That was approximately what Hurley said.)

Some time during the night the snow stopped falling and the wind died down. It remained cloudy in Washington the following day—the day of the parade and other inaugural activities.

It was bitterly cold along the banks of the Potomac on January 20, 1961. We were shivering in the freezing weather most of the day. The weather bureau later revealed the thermometer reached 18 degrees for a high that day. That was a damp cold that we couldn't seem to adjust to—not like our Arizona cold. Something called the "chill factor" must have made things worse than the thermometer indicated, because it was colder than the proverbial well-digger's hind end.

I'll say this for the snow-removal crews in Washington—they are efficient. About five or six inches of the white stuff had dropped on the capital city; not a bit of it remained on the parade route after the crew finished their job before the parade that day. There were, however, some icy spots along the route.

From early morning till after dark that night we impatiently awaited our turn to join the inaugural parade down Pennsylvania Avenue. The general plan was that the various parade entries were stationed in side streets and fed into the main stream of the parade as it made its way along, only it wasn't moving yet. We were waiting with several other entrants on our short side street and had been there since shortly after daybreak that morning. These side streets had not been cleared of snow. A Washingtonian had warned us at the motel that we'd better put on a lot of clothes because the weather forecast promised the day would be cold. I put on two sets of thermal underwear under my buckskins and before the day was over I wished I had on more.

Nearby, a contingent of pom pon girls from one of the area high schools was prancing and jumping around trying to keep warm. Those girls' legs were blue from the cold. A vendor of long-johns could have cleaned up in Washington that day. That was but one of many scantily-clad high school groups that should have stuck with their schedules of performing for athletic events at their respective schools where it was warmer. There were a lot of these groups sponsored by some congressman (or other nincompoop) who found it necessary to placate the voters back home. Add to that the lack of planning, timing, etc., of the parade officials and there was about as disorganized a parade as it could be possible to assemble. One news reporter we met lamented that oft-repeated phrase we were beginning to expect—"typical Washington thinking—and—" he added, "it's the same every four years."

We wished many times that day that the Phoenix J.C.s could be there to get that parade moving. Those guys know how to organize a parade!

The street we were on was lined with homes that looked warm and inviting. About the middle of the morning, a man came out of the nearest home carrying a large kettle of steaming coffee and a bundle of paper cups—"thought you fellows looked like you could use some coffee," said this samaritan. Right then I made one of the biggest mistakes I ever made (and I've made some lulus)—I forgot to get that man's name and address for a future, more formal, vote of thanks. Coffee was never so good or so welcome.

Everyone was stamping around in the snow to keep feet warm and circulation on the move—mount and dismount—anything to keep from freezing. Rod Graves, mounted at the time, swung his horse around sharply; the long rifle he had across his shoulders hit Gene Doyle on the side of the head and knocked him off his horse. Gene got to his feet—"I was just thinking it was about time to get off and stretch anyway—" he said, dusting the snow off.

We kept track of goings-on by various portable radios some of our neighboring groups had and relaying the information from group to group up and down the street. At noon we learned the president-elect and retinue of camp-followers were going to lunch and for two hours thereafter the populace would be regaled with speeches on varying subjects by varying personages. They would all be in a nice warm room, while we peasants would be out in the cold.

Someone (bless his thoughtfulness) brought back the bus that had brought us to the parade route earlier that morning. They, the horses, were stabled several miles away, in Maryland, and had to be transported by trucks to and from the parade route. I don't know what we'd have done without our wranglers—George Williams, Bob Dean and Louis Peters—they did a great job! I'd have frozen my hands for sure if I hadn't been wearing Bob Dean's gloves.

Half of our group stayed to look after the horses while the other half climbed aboard the bus and were trundled off to a place called Hall's, at 7th and K Streets, SW, on Washington's historic waterfront.

Hall's, according to the establishment's literature, had been host to famous celebrities and statesmen since 1885. They still maintained its "authentic 'turn-of-the-century' atmosphere with its gas lights, running water in the trough beneath the long Honduras mahogany bar." It was literally just that—a trough ran the full length under the bar with a continuous stream of water flowing past.

The big mural on the wall behind the bar drew much attention. That painting, supposedly scrutinized by many notables through the intervening years, also drew our attention. It was painted shortly after Hall's opened for business in 1885. This famous mural depicted the banishment of Adam and Eve from the Garden of Eden. In keeping with the theme, these life-sized subjects, of course, neither owned nor wore clothing—not even a fig leaf.

We lunched and refreshed ourselves. The place did have a modern touch: a TV set was tuned to the inaugural ceremonies. While we watched, a Cardinal, a close friend of the Kennedys, went to the lectern to give the invocation and start proceedings—there we'd been waiting all morning in the cold and the parade hadn't even started yet!! More of that Washington thinking conjured up by our nation's masterminds. While those plutocrats—bureaucrats—or whatever kind of crats they are (we had some good names for them) sat or stood around where it was warm, we were out in the cold.

Everyone who viewed that TV program that day remembers how, as the Cardinal spoke, a billow of smoke came out of the innards of that lectern thus causing concern among those who were near the scene. Gun-shy people started to move away from the vicinity. Ever since Abe Lincoln was shot, people have had an aversion for being in proximity to a president when something suspicious occurs. Everybody near that TV in Hall's at the moment heard Everett Coffee's appropriate remark concerning the smoking lectern where the concerned Cardinal was supplicating the Deity to pour down His blessing.

"Holy smoke," said Everett.

That smoke cloud was later revealed to have been caused by a short circuit in the electrical system. After the smoke cleared, they finally got the new president sworn in and we went back to the parade route so the other half could go to Hall's to rest and refresh themselves and ogle the mural on the wall.

Among our trappings we had two travoises. Our mascot Tuffy was a cub lion about one-third grown. He was in a cage on one travois that was hitched to a horse. My place in the parade was on a second travois. I was a wounded mountain man; I had an arrow that appeared to be sticking in my gizzard where some mythical Indian had shot me. When a parade started I laid on the travois and tried not to move too much so as to give the appearance of either being dead or wounded. If it got much colder I wouldn't have to act the part—I'd be too cold to move.

While impatiently awaiting our turn to join the parade, Tuffy became interested in the tail of the horse in front of him. He reached an investigative paw between the bars of his cage and started combing the hair in that tail. By stretching to the full extent of his reach the cub could reach the tantalizing tail. It became a game; the horse switching his tail and the lion stroking the hair every time it came within reach. The horse was starting to get fidgety.

Just a fraction of an inch farther and, should Tuffy become a little more excited in his experimental search for new adventure, he might sink a claw into the meaty part of that tail. And that might be "all she wrote" to get one hell of an unexpected rodeo started down Pennsylvania Avenue. Horses don't like or trust lions—something had to be done and soon.

For a little while there was enough excitement to make us forget the cold weather. Finally, several men kept Tuffy in the

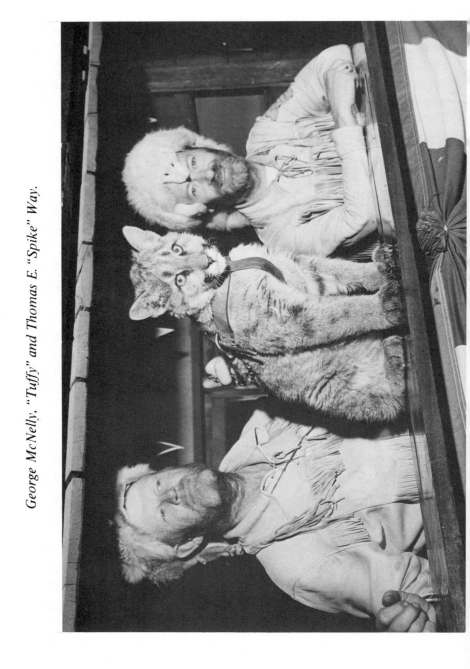

George McNelly, "Tuffy" and Thomas E. "Spike" Way.

back end of his cage by prodding him with rifle barrels (not even George McNelly, owner and keeper of the cub, wanted to interrupt Tuffy's reverie by getting his hands close to the cage). While Tuffy was being thus held off, Paul Tissaw fastened a board from my travois perch onto the front of the cage. Though this bit of strategy spoiled Tuffy's fun and games, the human element breathed easier. Our main worry then was "will that board hold?" Luckily it did.

The F.B.I. came around to check our long rifles to make sure they were inoperable. They were taking no chances that we might take a pot shot at the president or anyone else as we passed by on the parade route. It might not be beyond the realm of possibility that someone less civilized than we, who had been needlessly delayed in the cold environs of Washington that day might consider mayhem, or worse, should the opportunity arise.

While we were trying to keep warm, our two guest traveling companions from the Arizona Highway Patrol, Archie Morris and Harvey Golightly, were otherwise occupied. They pitched in to help the Washington police who were having a difficult time handling traffic along the parade route. Our patrolmen had been given special permission by the Highway Patrol to accompany us to Washington. At that moment, they were up to their necks unraveling traffic problems alongside the D.C. police. Score another round for Arizona! Archie Morris, a former cowboy and still a cowboy at heart, would rather have been back with us and the horses, cold as it was.

We did have one cold-induced casualty. On the night before the parade Jerry Duffield, then president of the group, developed a bad cold. Jack Greenway, who maintained the old Isabella Greenway King home in D.C., took Jerry home with him. Through timely care, the cold that threatened to turn into pneumonia was treated and Jerry was back with us again the night after the parade. He had watched the parade on TV at the Greenway home.

Some of us had been out to the Greenway home in the evening of our first day in Washington, before the storm. Isabella Greenway King, Jack's mother, had been a congress-woman from Arizona and the family had extensive property holdings in Arizona as well as in and around Washington.

Another casualty dated back before the parade—in Chicago. Somewhere in the shuffle of getting the men loaded on the Pennsy train when leaving the Windy City, a certain amount of horseplay was being indulged in. Somehow or other our guest, *Arizona Republic* correspondent, Bill Nixon, became the victim of an accident. Just how an innocuous-appearing powder horn could figure in such an accident I don't know; but at some point in the melee a flying powder horn stuck Bill below the right knee.

After limping that night and all the next day on a very sore leg, Bill went to the National Orthopedic Hospital in Arlington, Virginia, where an x-ray disclosed a fractured tibia. A doctor put the leg in a cast.

How he did it, I'll never know—but Bill hobbled around on that casted broken leg during the parade the next day taking pictures. The cast didn't cover the toes. They must have been cold in that freezing weather. That's what I call—"over and beyond" the duties of a press correspondent.

It was late in the afternoon before there was any parade activity near us or on that side street. Then, when it was nearly dark, entries started to move slowly out to join the parade. We were still a long way from Pennsylvania Avenue and farther yet from where the president was waiting for us.

Our outfit didn't get the green light till after dark that night. Arizona being the 48th state to be granted statehood, was almost at the end of the string. Only Hawaii and Alaska were behind us. Those gals from Hawaii had to shake up a new, faster cadence in their dance to keep warm—a brand new hula. The sled dogs from Alaska, however, felt right at home.

The TV crews had all packed their gear and left the parade route, due to darkness, long before we even got started down the "big avenue." And there went any chance the folks back home would have of seeing us on TV.

The Navajo Intertribal Band, as well as the White Mountain Apache Devil Dancers, all from Arizona, added color and drew well-deserved praise from the spectators along the parade route.

"It was the Bill Williams Mountain Men who will be the longest-talked-about entry in the smooth-shaven capital of the world..."enthused a reporter regarding Arizona's parade entries.

We finally went by the reviewing stand where the president had the place almost to himself. Most of those who had been there had moved inside where it was warmer—talk about rats deserting a sinking ship. We later learned that President Kennedy had told his associates and other assorted rats—oops—that, in spite of the cold he was going to stay and see "...those people who had traveled a long way to see me."

As we finally rode past the reviewing stand the president, according to the press, stated—"Well, look at this!" Then he got to his feet and roundly applauded our group. When I saw that, I was sorry I hadn't voted for him but vowed I would if he ran again for office. An assassin's bullet later deprived me of that privilege.

The *Arizona Republic* had this to say—"The Mountain Men bore their 'wounded' on a travois and on another travois they dragged a caged mountain lion to exhibit to the new president as they passed in review. Clearly, the boys from Williams were the top attraction of the colorful show as they slouched happily in their cold—cold saddles. The travois-born 'wounded' had a realistic arrow that appeared to pierce his giblets—etc.—"

And all sans TV.

Thurman and Mahala Mayes went to New York on vacation after our invasion of Washington was over. While in New York, Thurman was notified by the parade committee that we had won second place in the best marching division in the parade (Virginia Military Institute took first honors) and would he (Thurman) drop by to pick up the trophy. He opined he would be very happy to do so. He backtracked to Washington and laid claim to the three-foot-high trophy which he brought back home with him after vacationing in the east.

That trophy did much to assuage the hurt the lack of TV coverage had caused. We could forget and forgive, to a certain degree, the lack of concern held by the powers-that-be, namely the parade committee, but we still wonder—why can't they hold that parade earlier in the day and give everybody a fair shake at the publicity and a chance to get in out of the bitter cold of a January Washington night?

Typical Washington thinking?

* * * *

Four years later (January 1965) we again invaded Washington, D.C. to take part in the inaugural ceremonies. This time Lyndon Johnson was being sworn in as the president and Hubert Humphrey as vice-president.

This time we went by air, flying out of Phoenix via American Airlines. Rather than shipping our horses we rented a string of horses from an outfit that furnished rodeo stock to various rodeos. They were wintering at their headquarters in New Jersey after the rodeo circuit had closed for the season. These horses were perfect for our purposes; their uncropped manes were long and their ragged looking uncurried winter coats would fit our needs to a "T." This company furnished saddles and other tack and would truck the horses to the place the parade formed. After the parade they would pick the horses up at the end of the parade route. The price of this service would be considerably less, and much more convenient, than the cost and trouble of shipping our stock from Arizona. With all of that off our minds, we headed for Phoenix and Sky Harbor Airport.

The roll call of those making this air trek to Washington was: Ben Fillmore, Denton "Diz" Dean, Bill Evans, Jerry Duffield, Oscar Skaggs, Leo Black, Bill Lilly, Paul Tissaw, Ed Musgrove, George Tissaw, Bill Freeman, Pete Miller, Hurley Wright, Bill Wilson, Ray Gardner, Jim Barber, John Maillie, Dale Blood, Thomas "Spike" Way and Bill Sutton. Thurman Mayes and Martin C. "Doc" Flohr, with their wives, had gone on ahead and met us in Washington. As in our first inaugural trip, our good friend Bill Nixon, of the *Arizona Republic,* again accompanied us and again did a bang-up job of it.

It seemed like we had just cleared the Phoenix pattern when it was time to land at Tucson. That's where our airplane

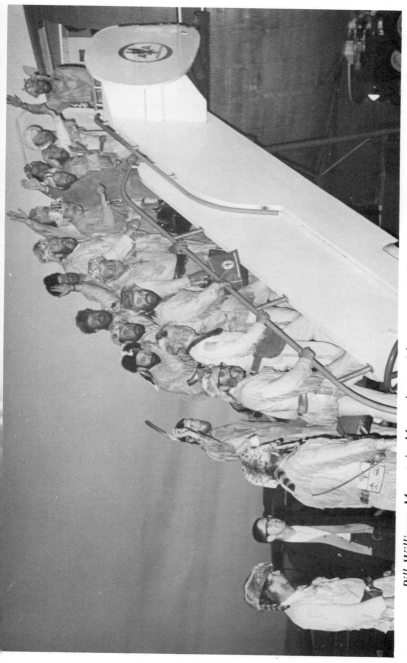

Bill Williams Mountain Men, along with reporter Bill Nixon (dark overcoat), board plane for Washington, D.C. in 1965.

developed trouble in the landing gear. We had gotten on the ground okay when the brakes on one side partially locked, causing the plane to veer from its course in a wide semi-circular path down the runway. Metal shavings from the multi-wheel bearings marked the course of our landing plane.

That, of course, rendered that plane *hors de combat.* Another 727 was flown in from San Diego on which we, after a three-hour delay, continued our journey. First, however, the crippled

At 39,000 feet, "Spike" Way and Bill Freeman met stewardess Carol Rothrum.

plane had to be unloaded and then everything reloaded on the replacement plane.

Hurley Wright walked out along the landing strip and studiously examined the metal (babbitt) shavings marking the path of our incoming plane. He had been skeptical from the start about the safety of airplanes and this incident did absolutely nothing toward allaying his already shaky distrust of that mode of travel. After all, no self-respecting mountain man should ever forsake his trusty horse or mule for one of those modern gadgets that leaves *terra firma* to fly like a bird. At that time, Hurley would have told you—"flying is for the birds!"

We finally convinced him that we didn't have time to horseback it to Washington. Reluctantly, he boarded the plane with us. There was a small jump seat near the main exit which is used by a stewardess during takeoffs and landings. Hurley eyeballed that seat and mentally figured, I am sure, the distance from there to the exit. Before takeoff, he managed to stray away from that seat to another in the passenger section where he tolerated the trip. I guess he finally got it figured out that one seat is no safer than another in case of a disaster. By the time the journey was over, he was a seasoned flier with a renewed respect for that method of travel—I think—?

Among our paraphernalia there were some bulky objects—packsaddles, a knocked-down travois, to be assembled later when needed. The travois had two long poles that took up a lot of space and were cumbersome. There were two large mule deer bucks that had been frozen solid; those deer had been taken in the previous fall season and frozen—then transferred to a Phoenix freezer locker. Before plane departure time they were taken from the freezer and loaded on the plane. These frozen carcasses would (and later did) add authenticity to our entry as they were borne by packhorses in the inaugural parade.

In the meantime, these frozen carcasses couldn't endure too great a delay between freezer and eventual parade. Fortunately, after clearing Tucson International Airport it was non-stop to Chicago. After a short stay at Chicago's O'Hare Airport, it was on to Washington non-stop.

We watched the baggagemen who unloaded our tack, deer,

etc., in Washington. They neither showed nor mentioned any unusual or foreign odor from the deer—we were still batting a thousand. In order to keep our batting average at a safe level we had the two carcasses stored by a local freezer company pending the parade.

On a Sunday morning, during our second Washington stay, we came out of our hotel, the name of which I can't remember. We were near one of those locations with which Washington abounds—streets like the spokes of a wagon wheel take off in all directions from the hub; we were close to the hub where there was a fish pond (empty that time of the year) and I believe some kind of a statue.

We noticed uniformed military guards stationed around a nearby church. Others, plainclothes and uniformed, all armed with rifles (we later learned they were secret service and treasury guards) were atop buildings in the surrounding area. Several of them had binoculars with which they scrutinized everything and everyone in sight. We, in our buckskins (even though we had left our muskets in the rooms) came in for a close examination; although at a distance—strictly eyeballing, no physical contact.

In due time, a procession of limousines and other vehicles headed by a squad of D.C. motorcycle police drove up to the church. President Johnson and his wife, followed by a group of camp followers and all flanked by bodyguards went into the church. Just a routine outing for our country's leader. It is peculiar that in this day and age we live in a country where we don't dare leave the president unguarded even for a minute, but I guess that's the way the cookie crumbles—the price of fame, as it were.

Later at the hotel Stewart Udall came to see us; he was then Secretary of the Interior and, of course, from Arizona.

We visited Arlington National Cemetery where we again watched the spectacular changing of the guard ceremony. We also visited the grave of President Kennedy, whose inaugural we had attended four years before. We felt he had been our friend.

On the lighter side we spent considerable time, and money, in the Speakeasies; there were two Speakeasies—honest, that was the real name. Even though prohibition had been over for many years, these two places smacked of memories of the olden, golden (for the bootlegger) days of Prohibition. Two musicians, a banjo player and a pianist, rotated their playing from one place to the other—old time Dixieland music and well done.

Both places specialized in beer and peanuts. You threw the peanut shells on the floor. At that time the peanut shells were ankle deep and increasing fast. In the middle of the room, on the ceiling there was a trapeze where, at times, a scantily-clad girl would swing back and forth. Before our crowd could get beyond ogling the trapeze and the girl, we were warned that the trapeze would not accommodate anyone heavier than slightly more than a hundred pounds. These dad-gummed mountain men were checking to see who among them was a lightweight to be hoisted up on the swing. Nobody qualified.

It was in one of those Speakeasies that we met some members of a group similar to ours, called the Montana Mountain Men. They had one behemoth of a member who allowed as how he was just about the champion beer guzzler of his neck of the woods (Montana) and probably the whole wide universe. He forthwith challenged us to bring forth our finest gladiator who indulged in that important pastime in order to arrange a contest to decide the issue and declare a champion of the two groups—or maybe the world. Apparently some sort of honor was deemed to be at stake.

The guy looked at Hurley Wright. Hurley was no midget by any standard of bulk, nor was his capacity for storing away the amber brew lacking in any way; at the moment he happened to be working seriously on a pitcher of the fluid in question. He sized up the denizen of the Montana wilderness who apparently was laying his mythical championship open to anyone who wished to contest his claim. At the moment his obvious wish was to hold an immediate suds-quaffing bout with our top qualified entrant, namely Hurley.

"I'm working on a helping of the stuff right now," said Hurley, "but," he said, "we might get together later."

Old Bill Williams would have found it difficult to pass up a challenge like that; entertainment was scarce in the old days.

Times have changed. Hurley had misgivings about any beneficial attribute being forthcoming from such a useless contest. "I don't mind insulting my kidneys a little," he said, "but enough is enough."

The gentleman from Montana and Hurley never consummated the so-called contest as far as I know. The self-proclaimed champion of the beer-ingesting circuit had to settle for a sociable evening among the two groups of mountain men.

The day of the parade was warm—quite a change from the cold miserable weather of four years before. There was no snow on the ground. A bus took us from our hotel across town to a place near the Capitol where trucks had already delivered the horses and tack to the area designated for our use. The two frozen deer and the knocked-down travois were brought to us by prearrangement with a driver for the freezer company.

Thurman Mayes and Paul Tissaw selected horses to haul the travois and the packs. The deer had been frozen in a form-fitting "U" shape which, when inverted, would conform to the packsaddles on the horses and thus they assumed the appearance of the freshly-killed camp meat they were supposed to resemble.

Much later, after the parade was over, the deer were given to the Washington Zoo. The day-long exposure to the warm weather had not been conducive to the preservation of the meat. The partially frozen carcasses, after thawing, would be a treat for the carnivorous animals of the zoo. There was no way we could take them back to Arizona—time and distance were not in our favor. In addition to the deer we also left the travois in Washington. The air freight cost would have been prohibitive to ship it back; we could always build another for future parades.

Back to the parade preparations—the horses acted as if nothing unusual was afoot. The packhorses all took to their new role very well. I guess it's second nature with knowledgeable cowhands like Thurman and Paul to know by looking at horses what the capabilities of the animals are. Then, too, these horses were trained to handle various jobs in the world of rodeo. I recall in the '40s one Bob Hansel furnished stock for our Williams rodeos. He had a pair of matched grey horses that pulled a wagon in the pre-rodeo parade. After the parade he pulled the harness off and put them in the string of bucking horses—and they were good buckers, too.

We had a few anxious moments after my travois was fastened to another horse. That horse had been picked by Paul as probably the most likely horse for the job. Poles rubbing on the sides of a horse are something else and we didn't know how this horse would like it; if he took a dim view of the situation we'd have to look for another horse. Seems like we worried for nothing; the strange contraption latched on him didn't bother him a bit.

The bus driver had stopped at an "oasis" along the way earlier that morning where most of us had purchased small vials of a cold remedy liquid to stave off the effects of a cold due to a possible change in the weather. If the weather remained warm the remedy could be used to combat snakebite, fatigue—the maladies are endless.

The horse Paul picked for himself was a lively animal and Paul had his hands full for a time, but it didn't take long to find that the horse was not in charge of the situation. Paul not only kept his horse under control but also had the horse pulling the travois under complete control. By the time the parade got underway both horses acted like they had been doing that task all their lives. The other horses seemed to fit into place and all was well as we headed for Pennsylvania Avenue.

That, however, was the calm before the storm. We were soon thereafter reminded that the normal life-style of these horses was rodeoing. Many of them were bucking horses, when a flanking strap was applied. Somewhere up ahead on a side street the Longhorn band of the University of Texas, according to correspondent Bill Nixon—"sounded a downbeat that shook the hallowed halls of Congress."

The rodeo was on. George Tissaw was unseated, but not hurt; Bill Lilly's horse tried unsuccessfully to climb into Bill Freeman's saddle with him; Freeman was carrying the American flag and the staff almost skewered John Maillie in the brisket. Eventually, however, order was restored—the horses quieted down and the parade continued.

Paul was a showman—a typical ham actor. With a receptive

audience along the parade route he occasionally gigged his mount in the flank to make him cut up, knowing just how far to goad the animal. I had a few anxious moments on my perch on the travois, but everything turned out well with no accidents.

This time around the weather was considerably warmer than it had been during the 1961 parade. It did, however, turn colder before the parade was over, making the two sets of thermal underwear under the buckskins feel welcome. My having to resemble a badly wounded or dead mountain man made it imperative that I lie still or reasonably so; I couldn't move around like the rest of them to keep warm. This time the weather made it easier to play dead.

As stated elsewhere, the long exposure of the frozen deer to the warm day was not conducive to the preservation of the venison, but it felt good to us in that parade—almost like Southern Arizona.

It was dark, just like four years before, when we finally got to see the president. This time the presidential reviewing stand was enclosed in bullet-proof glass and the enclosure was heated. The glass seemed to have a magnifying quality, bringing those inside closer to us. This bullet-proof enclosure was a precaution brought on by the recent assassination of President Kennedy, or so we were told.

Inside and out bright lights lit up the entire area. TV could have, but did not, cover the scene—Washington thinking?

As in the previous trip past this point, most of the crowd had deserted the presidential party. As my travois was hauled past I thought I'd add a little life to the party. I raised up, arrow and all, and waved at President Johnson.

Vice-president Hubert Humphrey poked the president in the arm and gestured—"look, it's Goldwater!"

While Humphrey applauded, the president waved back at me. The press made quite a to-do about the incident.

For our return home we were bussed to Baltimore where we enplaned for the trip back to balmy Arizona—tired from the trip but happy.

Another unforgettable rendezvous was history.

Our Luck Wasn't All Good

"nine years of bad luck in one ride!"

The 1962 rendezvous ride started out in about ten inches of snow with the thermometer hovering between fifteen and twenty degrees above zero. As the ride progressed our luck steadily went from bad to worse.

As Thurman Mayes, trail boss, later said—"I don't know what else could have gone wrong—we've had nine years of bad luck on this one ride." This was the ninth annual ride of the Bill Williams Mountain Men.

C. T. Mullen, one of our guests, brought along two horses for the trek. He planned to alternate between the horses; to ride one the first day and the other the next, and so on. Both were good horses that C. T.'s family rode occasionally around home— family pets that led a pampered life, soft living which might not be conducive to participating in a trail ride of this nature. But by alternating the riding there would be a minimum of work on them, as one then the other would be "empty" and loafing along was an ideal set-up for the horses—neither would have to work too hard. But the best made plans often go astray.

On the second morning, at Perkinsville, Everett Coffee approached C. T. with—"how about me riding your other horse?"

On a trail ride of this sort everyone more or less follows a pre-arranged trail as worked out by the trail boss. No matter how cut and dried the course is, there are many short cuts and other deviations from the main intended course.

There is considerable rough, rocky terrain along the upper Verde from Perkinsville down to Clarkdale, particularly around Sycamore Canyon; the latter area has been designated a wilderness area. In this area Coffee found himself on a rocky ledge that ended abruptly against a rock wall of the canyon. Instead of getting off and/or backing the horse a few feet to where he could be turned around to go back, Coffee forced the horse off the ledge, a drop of some four or five feet, to the loose

Mountain Man George McNelly

rocky shale-like formation of the slope below. There was apparently a cleft or obstruction under the loose dirt where a hoof caught and the momentum of the animal snapped the leg bone. The horse almost went down, but recovered and slid the several feet to the bottom of the incline.

The very pronounced limp of the horse was discovered to be due to a break above the right front fetlock.

The cook had a .38 caliber revolver in his duffel, which he dug out and offered to C. T. It was a forlorn sight to see C. T. lead that limping horse, later in the evening, up an arroyo out of sight. Later the sound of a gunshot broke the stillness of the gathering darkness.

That night we camped at Cloverleaf Ranch, several miles above Camp Verde, where, during the night, about four inches of snow dropped on us. Early the next morning we took out for Bumblebee where we would be down under the snow belt. As we neared the mountains' crest on the western side of the valley, there was ice on the road and a cold wind to make us keep our jackets on. Our cook trailer ran into trouble while going up Copper Canyon Hill when a car skidded into it, bending an axle on the trailer.

The noon stop was made shortly after we topped out of Copper Canyon Hill near where I-17 emerges from the Verde Valley. Hopefully our luck would take a turn for the better—but it didn't.

We had two horse trailers along. After the horses had been grained and the men fed (the welfare of the horses was always our first consideration), we loaded two horses that we hoped wouldn't be needed that afternoon in a trailer I was pulling. I took out for Bumblebee, where I unloaded them in a corral at our night campsite. I then doubled back along the road in case of stragglers who might need a ride or to haul crippled horses or those otherwise in need of a rest along the way.

There were still some extra horses along with the riders. These extra mounts, after the first few hours of the first day, keep up with the riding group without having to be led. It doesn't take long for them to realize that they get their hay and grain the same as the rest of the horses. They are not going to stray far away from the group for the balance of the trip. By the second day you'd have difficulty in driving the loose horses away from the herd; they assume a sort of camaraderie not unlike that trait in people.

Not long after I had started for Bumblebee, a second trailer loaded with two horses had started for the same destination. One of these horses was a big gelding belonging to the Sharp family. Charlie Sharp had brought him along to give him an outing; he was a family pet. Charlie figured the exercise would be good for him. He rode him once in a while to rest his other horse.

I don't recall who was driving the pickup, but Leo Black was a passenger; it was from Leo that I got the story. Nearly a mile south of the present Cordes Junction, the highway starts downhill. Another couple of miles down the road is the turnoff to Cordes and at Cordes the dirt road (the old Black Canyon Highway) turns south and soon thereafter dips down into Black Canyon; thence to Bumblebee, Cleator and several worked-out mines of the area. That section of the road is a segment of the old stagecoach trail from Prescott to Phoenix (the original Black Canyon Highway).

These men with their cargo of horses had just started down the hill before coming to the Cordes turnoff. They braked a time or two to keep from gathering too much speed on the smooth blacktop. Looking out the left window, they observed a horse trailer slowly passing them. It looked familiar—

"My God, that's our trailer!" yelled the driver.

Sure enough, it was. Somehow or other, the hitch had not been secured properly or had worked loose and unhitched the trailer. There was no way of stopping it. The trailer was already on the shoulder of the road and headed for the ditch. It ran off the shoulder and into the ditch where it overturned, off the highway. One of the horses, although shaken-up and frightened, was unhurt aside from a triangular-shaped tear in the hide on one shoulder.

It took some doing, but the horse was loaded into my trailer. I trailered him to Bumblebee where Doc Flohr later sewed up the loose flap of hide, amid remarks of a few characters who laughingly suggested that he hang out his shingle as a veterinarian. Doc responded with—"you jackasses get in line and wait your turn."

The other horse in the wrecked trailer, belonging to Charlie Sharp, suffered a broken back and had to be destroyed.

I didn't envy C. T. and Charlie their position. They were confronted with the sad task of informing their families of the tragedies that had befallen their pets. These were not just horses—they were both "part of the family."

In another rendezvous ride, trouble of another nature overtook us. Along the East Verde in the Seven Springs vicinity there were soft mud deposits of almost the consistency of quicksand. These spots make crossing the river a treacherous undertaking in several areas known only to local ranchers. We were warned not to ford the river except at regular crossings, some of which, but not all, were well marked.

It was about the middle of the afternoon when the main group came to the river, a river that showed no signs of the danger lurking in the shallow water flowing gently past. A local rancher had joined the group a short distance back and rode along to point out a safe crossing.

The main group, guided by the rancher, crossed the river and headed downriver following a trail that paralleled the river. A half-mile or more down the river was where Oscar Skaggs, who was for some reason lagging behind (the riders were usually strung out over a mile or more), caught up; only he was on the wrong side of the river. He plunged his horse in the shallow water and started across to join the main group. He didn't get far. His horse was soon in trouble, floundering in the soft mud or quicksand.

When the episode started, it looked like big trouble, so we set up camp for the night nearby. It was well that we did; there was a tough and time-consuming job involved in rescuing the horse. It took until about nine o'clock that night to extricate the very frightened animal from the mire. The horse was trailered the balance of the trip. Though that animal recovered to an extent from the experience, he would never again be the same as before

It's siesta time for (l. to r.) Gene Mason, George McNelly and Hurley Wright.

his baptism in quicksand.

On another trip, trouble of another nature overtook us, that is, one of our guests. Old John Barleycorn moves in mysterious circles. This guest, while feeling no pain, due to a more than generous acquaintanceship with the cup that cheers, was approaching our night campsite near Humboldt. The camp was set up inside a small pasture. The entrance was by way of a gate and adjoining cattleguard. The gate was open for our use.

As usual, when our camps were near a highway we had lots of company. At this Humboldt camp several carloads of people had stopped to see who we were, what we represented, and so on.

The incoming roistering guest rider had noticed the small group of visitors and was going to make a grand entrance to entertain the crowd. The open gate was ignored by the *vaquero* who was bent on displaying his prowess as a horseman. His reasoning, or lack of same, would have him jump his horse across the cattleguard—that should be good for a round of applause—

With a wild whoop and the application of spurs, this "cowboy" drove his mount forward. The horse did not co-operate; he lunged forward but slid to a stop at the edge of the cattleguard. The hapless rider, after a futile attempt to hang on, fell in an inglorious heap on the ground at the horse's feet. The horse had sensed the danger, but his momentum had taken him too far—one forefoot was caught between two rails in the cattleguard.

Heavy iron bars, borrowed from a nearby mining company, were used to spring the rails enough to get the foot out. The horse had stood quietly for almost three hours while that was going on; he knew that, had he tried to move, the leg might be broken—a liberal application of horse-sense such as the rider did not have. The leg was swollen but not broken. Liberal use of horse liniment and rest would be in order. The horse was trailered to his home pasture in Phoenix the next day.

On another trip, Bill Sutton had a close call in an accident. On the first day of the trip, shortly before the noon stop, several riders were passing a small water hole at the side of the road. Bill decided his horse needed a drink, so he reined the animal over to the water hole.

The deepest part of the pond was scarcely a foot in depth, which was fortunate for Bill as things turned out. As it is in many small lakes in this area, the sides and bottom were silted over from the runoff of many rains. Consequently, the bottom was covered with a deep coat of mud. This causes a slippery footing in places, in other places a hoof can sink in and can be extricated only with difficulty. The horse stepped in such a place and started to slide, after he finally freed his foot.

Bill tried to get off, but didn't make it. The horse went down, pinning Bill underneath. His companions got Bill and his horse, both covered with mud, out of the mess with difficulty. By the time they reached noon camp everyone was joking about the incident—even Bill. Just another trail hazard that was alleviated by a generous portion from the cup that cheers. After getting wet, you have to ward off a cold or pneumonia—you know, strictly the medicinal value of the stuff.

Many calamities were narrowly averted as these rendezvous trips continued through the years. Many riders claimed a miraculous cure for most anything and everything was effected by the internal application of Old Barleycorn; as our neighbors to the south might say—*quien sabe!*

Around the Cook Fire

dog-gone good "stew"

Ever since our umbilical cord was severed we've tried to keep body and soul together by way of the stomach and what we put in it. That surgical maneuver had been done a long time ago but we were still a little finicky about what went into our gullets; therefore, our search for cooks centered around picking the best available Dutch oven cooks.

There are many who know their way around a modern kitchen, but on the trail we were a long way from a kitchen stove. Not everyone understands Dutch oven cookery, but we always managed well in our choice of cooks. Everyone in the club could, and did on occasion, pitch in to help the cook, if he needed help.

Our camp cooking set-ups ranged from very primitive to quite complete. The first year we had everything on one pickup, which made for a very awkward situation. About the time the campsite for the night was found and we had partially unloaded, it was time to go back up the trail with liquid refreshment for the troops, some of whom were scattered over several miles. Then rush back where the cook had been left at the camp. The chuck wagon box, with the utensils, etc., was still on the pickup. If there was to be a next year's trip in our future, we were going to need a different set-up.

If anyone expected to see a menu of quail under glass or beef with bordelaise sauce to choose from, he was either in the wrong camp, or he had loitered too long at the beer truck sharpening his appetite for the onslaught on the next meal. Although the food wasn't tagged with a fancy name, it was wholesome, good and plentiful. The first couple of years we had beefsteaks and fried potatoes up to our ears—there wasn't time enough to cook much of anything else.

After the first year, our cooks had more time to devote to the preparation of meals. By then we used more vehicles on the trip. The novelty of "riding horseback all the way" had lost some of its luster and we had plenty of drivers. Some of us traded off occasionally between riding and driving. From the start, this trek was never intended to be an endurance contest.

One morning, Paul got up before the cook did (beer will do that to you). The first thing on the agenda that early in the morning, before daylight, was to build the fire and get the coffee pot on to boil. There were no fancy coffee makers or percolators. There was a big two-gallon pot, blackened from many camp fires, which was brought into use. Standard procedure in camp life where modern measuring devices are at a premium; you put one small handful or about a heaping tablespoonful (as near as you can guess) of coffee per one cupful of water in the pot. The water is not measured a cup at a time—like the coffee, the amount of water is subject to guesswork. After the coffee boils, you move the pot off the fire where a few hot coals will keep it hot. Then you toss a cup of cold water in the kettle to settle the grounds and you're in business.

Paul had hands as big as good-sized hams; needless to say, that coffee was as strong as varnish remover. When the pot contents got down toward the bottom, more water was added, but no more coffee. Then the stuff would still curl your hair— which wouldn't affect a couple of our members.

"Any of you fellows notice the coffee was kinda weak this morning?" complained Jake January.

"Tomorrow, you make it," grumped Paul, "maybe you'll do better."

Good-natured complaining and bantering continually added to the camaraderie of the group; kidding was the order of the day. Paul went on to explain:

"Reminds me—a fellow over along Cherry Creek was telling an eastern visitor one time how to make coffee. He said he often had to shove a few cows aside to dip the coffee pot in the water hole to get the water—even, on occasion, he shoved cow-droppings on the water to one side. Then he explained—'with your pot almost full of water, pick the sticks, grass and cow-droppings (not his exact wording) out, then you throw in a helluva lot of coffee—no trick at all to makin' coffee.' "

Sometimes we had to haul it a long distance, but we always had clean water on our sashays to rendezvous.

The cook finally had a chuckwagon separate from the other units and unencumbered with bed rolls, etc. A different truck hauled bedrolls. Another hauled hay and grain. It eventually worked out that the portable bar was a separate unit altogether. That meant less grumbling in the ranks and less aggravation for the cook.

Those who drove trucks were constantly on the lookout for dry hardwood for the cook fire; oak in the high country, driftwood along the Verde and mesquite in the lower elevations. Dry hardwood made much less smoke.

Much later we had a regular traveling kitchen built on a trailer chassis. There were gas plates to cook on—even a gas water heater. All the comforts of home. Until then, all cooking was done on an open fire.

I've been around several cooks on various trips. They ranged from good to better. All of them knew their way around the cook fire and could put together a meal that would satisfy anyone. One year our cook made rice pudding in a Dutch oven that was the best, by far, that I've ever eaten. Of course, when you're out in the fresh air all day everything has a tendency to taste better.

A few words of warning about Dutch oven cookery in general. Due to having hot coals not only under the oven, but also on top, great care must be taken when lifting the lid off; otherwise you might have ashes in the cookin'.

We sometimes had biscuits three times a day. The bunch got out early in the morning and wanted a stick-to-your-ribs breakfast that would hold them till noon. Along with the bacon, eggs and hash browns, they devoured biscuits and gravy in large amounts. Even those who ate very little breakfast at home ate like half-famished wolves on this trip.

Biscuits are made in the opened top of a sack of flour that has been set where it won't be accidentally knocked over. Scoop out a hole in the flour, banking the loose flour around the hole; pour the liquid mixture into the hole. With a big spoon scrape the flour, a little at a time, and work it into the mixture until the dough picks up enough flour to be the right consistency. Then take the dough out and put it on the floured work board and finish up by kneading and rolling it out with a rolling pin or beer bottle. Break off hunks of dough and form into biscuits (if you don't have a biscuit cutter, which we didn't at first) then put them into the hot Dutch oven. Then, with hot coals under and scooped on top, it won't take long to cook them. Tie up the top of the flour sack and you're through.

Sharing a relaxing moment on the trail ride are (l. to r.) Bill Lilly, C. T. Mullen, "Spike" Way and Paul Tissaw. (They did not wear buckskins all the time.)

I was particularly interested as, by using this method there was one less pan to wash. I don't know who thought of it, but we cut both ends out of a small can that chili peppers came in and—presto—we had a biscuit cutter for the next batch of biscuits.

In answer to your unasked question—the liquid will not penetrate the flour in that sack any farther than what you stir into it. Camp cooks have used this fool-proof method since way back. The dough lifts out in a lump, leaving dry flour in the sack.

Did you ever try to flip a flapjack in a deep Dutch oven? If you have you'll understand why pancakes were replaced by biscuits for breakfast—biscuits and gravy, that is. The thick white gravy served up by the cook has a very uncomplimentary name in cow-camp lingo, which does not detract from its edibility. Mighty good grazing.

With the new cook-trailer a few years later and gas cookery, a griddle could be used for making pancakes. I remember only once in my twelve years with the group where pancakes were made. The old Dutch ovens were still indispensable to our older school of cooks, as was the popularity of biscuits and gravy.

A camp cook is as hard to get a recipe out of as your Aunt Jerusha or any other old-time cook. They never measured anything, that is, by any understandable medium. It was always—"a dab of this—a smidgen of that—a pinch of something—a dollop of something else—" after that—"a good-sized hunk of meat—then you use a big pinch, or two or three shakes of salt—a couple shakes of pepper, etc." Some things— "need a goodly amount of cookin'—" Some should be cooked— "just a mite—"

You can't miss—just follow those directions. These cooks mean well and really are telling you how to make your favorite dish, even if you can't decipher—"a pinch—a dollop—" and so on.

I remember one day we got settled with camp set up early in the afternoon, near Humboldt. Bill Freeman suggested that we have baked potatoes for supper that night. Bill and I did a lot of camp duty on some of these trips. We picked out about twenty pounds of medium-sized spuds, washed them, wrapped them in foil, then tossed them in the hot coals—a fire had already been started. Next we put a thin layer of dirt on top, then more fire and coals on top of that.

By supper time the potatoes were done. Only about half of them were used that night. We cut open and scooped out the rest of them and made hash browns of them the next morning for breakfast. I never tasted any better hash browns anywhere.

On these trips we always ate good food and lots of it. There was, however, a noticeable lack of salads but always a plentiful supply of meat (mostly steaks) and potatoes.

At the end of the trips we stayed in motels and ate in restaurants "just like the folks uptown." One day we managed to get past the bar and into the restaurant at the Bali Hi Motel. Hurley Wright expressed the opinion, shared by many of us, after we got seated. He looked around and said—"after steaks three times a day all week, it sure is great to look at and eat one of these chef's salads." There was a groan of approval around the table. Lack of refrigeration facilities, of course, prohibited lots of things we might have otherwise enjoyed.

One of our members, Jerry Duffield, usually cooked the pinto beans for the barbecues we put on from time to time to replenish our treasury. The Duffield family had been in the sheep and cattle business during Jerry's formative years, so it was quite natural that he learned the fundamentals of sheep and cow-camp cookery. His cooking experience was not confined to making beans palatable for the public. He learned the sometimes complicated art of Dutch oven cookery; how to cook such rangeland concoctions as "mountain oysters" and "sonofabitch."

The parts that are removed from a bull calf in the process of neutering the animal are considered a delicacy. The mountain oysters (prairie oysters, if you are a flatlander) in the older days were tossed on the hot coals of the branding fire to roast. These rangeland *hors d'oeuvres* were alleged to be a special treat.

By prearrangement with Jerry, some of our J. C. friends from Phoenix brought a bucket of these tidbits up from a meat packing plant. Jerry cooked them by boiling them for a while, then roasting them in the oven. I tried a couple and, frankly, my considered opinion of this gastronomic delicacy was that they should have been left on the calf, but most of the guys like them.

As to the other epicurean delight—sonofabitch (pronounced just like it looks): various cooks through our first years on the trail had threatened to cook a sonofabitch but nobody did in any of the years I was in the club. Jerry said that the meat packing plants should have a "packaged deal" containing most of the required ingredients and that he would check with them. He did and they did (have them, that is).

The English have their tripe, made from the stomach and various entrails of an animal. In Scotland there is a popular dish called haggis, made from calf or sheep hearts, livers, lungs and small intestines, mixed with suitable seasonings, and boiled in the animal's stomach. The sonofabitch, strictly Western American in origin, uses the marrow (milk) gut (thoroughly cleaned) from the intestines. The other ingredients of this famous dish of the West (all edible when used singly) are the kidneys, brains, sweetbreads, heart and liver.

Before Jerry's restaurant opened (it had been closed for remodeling), he cooked up the *piece de resistance* (sonofabitch) for the mountain men and their wives. Almost everyone guessed that the concoction was alright, but they were a little less than enthused when offered a second helping.

The dish was said to have originated in early roundup camps of the West. When setting up camp, a calf or young steer was immediately butchered out and the meat hung up to set and cool for "camp meat." Undoubtedly, some enterprising cook wondered what to feed a bunch of hungry cowboys while the meat was cooling out and figured out the sonofabitch. Sheep camps have their own version of this dish, the ingredients being taken from a lamb rather than a calf.

All the foregoing ingredients are cut in small pieces. The cooking process entails considerable time, starting with the marrow gut. It is boiled several hours, then the other ingredients are added and the entire conglomeration boils for several more hours. Seasonings—salt, pepper, garlic, chile, etc., are added when almost done. If it is thin or soupy, add a little flour to thicken. If individual taste dictates, and it often does, various vegetables may be added. Vegetables, however, are not usually considered a part of the (oh—oh—that word again).

That whatchamaycallit somewhat resembles a stew when done. However, to label it "stew" brands one as a dude. One old timer irately suggested—"there is one and only one name for it—a sonofabitch. It has always been that and always will be. To refer to it as a 'stew' detracts from something that's in a class by itself." Perhaps the *nom-de-plume* "stew" was intended to take some of the sting out of the name and make it more acceptable to delicate ears.

Just how the concoction got its name is debatable—there are many versions—just as the list of ingredients may vary with the cook and the locality.

A variation of this dish is found in a diary written by a member of the Lewis and Clark Expedition, at Milk River, under date of Thursday, May 9, 1805. Using the author's original spelling, it follows:

"I killed one buffaloe and we saved the necessary materials making what our cook Charbono calls the 'Bondin Blanc' or white pudding." (Toussaint Charbonneau was a cook and guide for the Lewis and Clark Expedition.)

"About six feet of the lower extremity of the large gut of the buffaloe is the first morsel that the cook makes love to. This he holds fast at one end with the right hand, while with the forefinger and thumb of the left he gently compresses and discharges what he says 'is not good to eat.'

"The mustle lying underneath the shoulder blade next to the back and fillets are next sought. These are needed (kneaded) up very fine with a good portion of kidney suit (suet); to this composition is then added a just proportion of pepper and salt and a small quantity of flour.

"Then Charbono siezes his recepticle which has never once touched water, for that would destroy the order of the procedure.

"The operator seizes the recepticle I say, and tying it fast at one end turns it inward and begins now with repeated evolutions of the hand and a brisk motion of the finger and thumb to put in what he says is 'bon pour manger' (good to eat); thus by stuffing it drives from the other end of the recepticle a much larger portion of the (blank place in the manuscript) than was previously discharged by the thumb and finger. It is tyed at the other end then baptised in the Missouri River with two dips and a flirt, and bobbed in the kettle; from whence after it be well boiled it is taken and fryed with bears oil until it becomes brown, when it is ready to esswage the pangs of a keen appetite or such as travelers in the wilderness are seldom at a loss for."

Sonofabitch, mountain oysters or *bondin blanc*—all are of Western origin. So far I haven't and have no desire to sample the *bondin blanc.*

Said one grizzled old-timer, "You ain't really lived till you've ate a sonofabitch—Ha!—a feast fit for the kings!" However, Western protocol notwithstanding, many cowboys don't care if the kings have it all. Some of these ornery cowpokes will just hang around and wait for the meat to cool. Whoops there pardner—don't put them cards away yet. Deal me another hand—I'll wait, too.

No dissertation on that subject (s.o.b.) would be complete without adding Johnnie Rogers' story. Johnnie was an old-timer who once cowboyed for the old C. O. Bar (Babbitts) in Northern Arizona.

It was roundup time. A beef had been butchered and the meat hung up to cool and set up. The cantankerous cook was going through the entrails and came out with the marrow gut when a particularly seedy-looking saddle tramp came by and stopped.

"Cookie, looks like you're gonna have a sonofabitch for supper," observed the drifter.

The crusty patriarch of the cook wagon bristled, glared at the intruder, then snarled—"looks like I'm gonna have two of 'em!"

True to the code of the West, that drifter was fed before he continued his journey. The cook's bark was much worse than his bite.

The Arizona Story

be-whiskered thespians

On Sunday, March 15, 1959, KOOL-TV (now KTSP) and the Phoenix Civic Light Opera Association presented what the press referred to as "television's first spectacular produced outside of New York or Hollywood." This spectacular covered 400 years of Arizona's history, from early Indian culture to the present time. Said the press—"The Arizona Story will touch on six major eras in the state's rich and colorful history."

As reasonably accurate facsimiles of the mountain men of old, we came under the scrutiny of the Phoenix Light Opera Association directors. The era of the mountain men was one of the phases of Arizona's past that, although brief in years and not overly abundant in numbers of beaver trapped, played an integral part in the civilization of the West.

They drafted three of us—Jerry Duffield portrayed Old Bill Williams, Oscar Skaggs was Kit Carson and I was James Ohio Pattie. Though somehow it seemed out of character, we managed to overcome our timidity and got in the spirit of the stage rendition—and enjoyed it!

The reason we were in Phoenix and had our whiskers was that we were in the last day (March 15) of our annual rendezvous. When the final rodeo performance was over that afternoon, the Bill Williams Mountain Men packed up and went home leaving we three "thespians" to the terrors of the stage. We each had only short speaking parts and only one rehearsal that afternoon, but we got by without any loss of memory—I think. The play was presented at ten that night, which of necessity delayed our departure from Phoenix until almost midnight. We got home in the wee hours of the next morning.

One of our first desires on getting home from rendezvous was a visit to our favorite barber. Our facial hirsute adornment had done its service until another year would roll around. That pleasure, however, was to be denied us temporarily.

The Williams Playmakers were putting on a pageant a few days hence—a Passion Play program in connection with the upcoming Easter season.

"We need your whiskers for our rendition," they explained, then added, "however, you can launder them for your comfort and well-being." I guess we did add not only color but aroma to the surroundings before we got out of our buckskins. We would, we were coaxed to say, "add our bit toward the festivities."

So it came to pass that we, in our humble manner, added to the overall atmosphere (no cracks please) of the play. Doc Flohr was also added to the cast. None of us had speaking parts. The play according to the *Williams News,* "has been loudly acclaimed by those who witnessed it."

I can still see Doc Flohr lying there in his toga on a pillow-bedecked couch with a slave girl dropping grapes in his mouth (what a life!). The rest of us, similarly robed, wandered aimlessly about adding our bit to the over-all decor of the production.

With that play over , our thespian ambitions came to an end. We shaved the next day and returned to our respective vocations, albeit somewhat buoyed by the thought that our whiskers had helped someone, despite the discomfort they had given us.

What's a barber to do?

We Go to Las Vegas

...a little drop in a...puddle

We made a trip to Las Vegas to appear in the HELLDORADO DAYS PARADE in May, 1959. This was an extracurricular ride and did not replace our regular annual rendezvous trip to the J. C.'s World's Championship Rodeo in Phoenix. In fact, we had made the annual Phoenix trek two months previously.

Paul Tissaw led the horseback contingent across country for a small part of the way, but most of the journey was made by trailer. We didn't have the necessary time for a prolonged trip so all, including the horses, had a nice ride in style.

Oscar Skaggs, Bill Evans and I met movie actress Linda Darnell at a bistro along the strip. Our buckskins were not the cleanest in the world so, to prevent the gamy aroma from reaching too far, we maneuvered downwind from the beautiful movie queen and her retinue of camp followers. We stopped at the entrance of the club and stared at her and her entourage as they approached. She was tired from long exposure to the gaping public and wanted to know what picture we were working on (buckskins and all, you know). We told her who we were, for what it was worth. We knew she was a movie actress but couldn't think which one, so we asked her who she was.

"I'm a sonofabitch if I know—," was her unexpected, tired, drawn out response. Then she said, "...Oh, I'm sorry—I'm Linda Darnell."

She was a heckuva nice person, as were those with her; they, however, kept an eye on us so we wouldn't get too close. It was some time later when we realized we should have asked for her autograph—but, then, a trio of country boys can't think of everything.

We had brought our bedrolls along and slept with the horses—they didn't seem to mind. I remember feeling as if I were coming down with a cold the next morning when I rolled out of the sack. Doc Flohr had brought along medical supplies for man and beast. Just then he was injecting strocillin (a type of penicillin) into several horses for something or other. I asked Doc if that stuff was good to fight a cold in a human, as was penicillin. He assured me it was. I assured him I was not allergic to penicillin.

"Get in line with the horses and drop your britches," said Doc, "the horses won't care." That's just what I did; I don't recall neighing as a result.

Good old Doc. I never saw anyone who enjoyed our trips any more than he did. He missed being a charter member by one year. Added to a growing list of our group, Doc has since gone to that last rendezvous where nobody will steal his traps or furs and he won't have to contend with freezing winters.

After the horses were all inspected and loaded and started on their journey back home, a couple of carloads of us stopped in at the Showboat for a final fling with the cards, et al.

Fred Theroux was having his way pretty much at a blackjack table—so much that the establishment changed dealers quite often. We kept gigging the dealers by telling them Fred could beat them at their own game (and he was doing just that) no matter how many dealers they warmed up in the bullpen. The management was glad to see us leave.

We were barely mentioned in the press for this Vegas venture. Had it been after one of our inaugural forays to Washington, we might have created more of a splash, but as it was we were a little drop in a big puddle. Our first presidential inaugural adventure was still two years in the future.

"Doc" Martin C. Flohr

The Smoki Dancers

dancers and "little brothers"

On the second night out on our trip to Phoenix in March 1959, we camped near Prescott. A large contingent of the Smoki People of Prescott came out to visit us. The Smokis are a group of white businessmen who have, through diligent research, study and training, become widely acclaimed for their accurate interpretations of Indian lore, particularly in the many ceremonial dances. Among the various dances is the Smoki rendition of the world-famous Hopi Snake Dance. From year to year different ceremonial dances are enacted by the Smoki, but the snake dance is perennially on their agenda.

The Smoki invited us to pow-wow with them at their club house in Prescott, an invitation we gladly accepted. They told us to bring our appetites along and transported us into town. We were entertained royally by the Smoki and their ladies with a never-to-be-forgotten banquet and accompanying libation. Before the "tribe" took us back to our camp that night they invited us to be their guests at their Annual Smoki Ceremonials a few months hence. Needless to say, we accepted with alacrity. That's why, on an early August evening in 1959, we were in the "sacred arena of the Smoki" in Prescott.

We were the only outsiders ever allowed inside the ceremonial grounds, or arena, during their ceremonial dances—just the Smoki, the snakes and the Bill Williams Mountain Men in full buckskin regalia. We, the mountain men, squatted in a group along the outer perimeter and had a ringside seat for the performances. We, of course, did not interfere in any way but tried to be as inconspicuous as possible in an effort to enact a scene of friendliness as in days gone by wherein white people intermingled freely with the friendly Indians. Our presence in such close quarters with that bunch of snakes, used in the portrayal of the widely-publicized Snake Dance might be attributed to the use of bullsnakes by the Smoki People, instead of the venomous rattlesnakes used by the Hopi Indians.

Bill Williams Mountain Men meet with the Smoki in Prescott.

We, the mountain men, held our ground very well until toward the end of the snake dance. At that time, the dancers released the "little brothers" (several bushels of lively bullsnakes) to carry the plea for rain to the rain gods. These slithering bearers of that important message wriggled in all directions, a move quickly emulated by the mountain men.

After the first shock, we realized the snakes were relatively harmless and we almost overcame our fear of them. We even fondled some of them, being careful not to single out the larger ones. We had seen what one of the larger reptiles did during the dance. One of the snake priests had one that was particularly active but suddenly became aggessive, scared, or, for some reason known only to a bullsnake, wrapped itself around the snake priest's arm and squeezed. That's the method used by a bullsnake, being a constrictor in nature's scheme, to kill its prey.

One of the other snake priests came to the rescue and helped calm and unwind the snake which eventually released its pressure. The dancers were old hands at the game and never missed a step in the dance. Except for an occasional such instance, we were told, the bull or gopher snake is a very friendly creature and makes a good pet and an excellent mouser around barns, chicken coops, etc.

After the dances, our families came down from the stands and joined us; however, they didn't get too close to the snakes that were still squirming around. These snakes were later gathered and taken out in the country where they were released in their native habitat.

My son Tom, age eight at the time, captured one of the smaller ones and wanted to take it home. He named it Jimmy, honoring one of our neighbors. He (Tom) reluctantly set "Jimmy" free after we explained we probably didn't have enough gophers at or around home to keep the snake furnished with a satisfactory diet.

Bill Evans likewise "took a likin'" to one of the larger of the "little brothers." Virginia had to talk long and convincingly to keep the not-so-little "little brother" from accompanying them back to Williams that night.

Tuffy

call of the wild!

George McNelly, being a rancher, naturally looked upon the mountain lion as a predator and, as such, a menace to his livestock. Rarely does any rancher pass up an opportunity to rid the area of another cat—big or little. Then, too, there is a bounty paid for the eradication of these "obnoxious critters"—just cut off the ears, present them to the right source and collect.

Cougar—puma—catamount—panther—mountain lion—choose the name that fits your own part of the country—he's the same big cat. Once I was attending a meeting in New Orleans with our local Civil Air Patrol unit. Several of us were lunching in an open-air restaurant when a man strolled past leading a full-grown mountain lion—cougar—on a leash.

"Look at the mountain lion," I said to nobody in particular.

"That there's a swamp cat," mumbled the obviously insulted man on the other end of the leash, "don't see no mountains around here, do ya?"

What's in a name? That animal is at home almost everywhere regardless of the *nom de plume* he travels under; he is also a predator in all of those locations.

Ever present in a stockman's mind is the thought that a little lion can grow up to be a big lion; big lions can pose a threat to the stockman's colts, calves, sheep, etc. That's why the following is a surprising twist in the behavior of one person who had no particular love for a predatory animal.

After a successful lion hunt wherein George McNelly and another hunter had "treed" and disposed of a large female lion, they noticed that the dead cat had been nursing a litter of cubs. They put the dogs on the scent and backtracked the lion's trail. Before long they found the den where three cubs were in residence; one of them was dead.

Ordinarily the young cats would have been summarily disposed of; however, George recalled a meeting of the Bill Williams Mountain Men club some time before. George was a member. The subject had come up concerning a mascot that would fit in with the *ambiance* of the club. The idea had been tossed around that perhaps a mountain lion would make an ideal and unusual mascot.

Instead of disposing of the cubs—they were cute little rascals—each of the hunters took a cub home with him to raise. The McNellys named their new pet Tuffy, a name that seemed to fit his actions.

As the little fellow grew from a cuddly little ball of fur—it didn't take long—into an overgrown version of a fluffy plaything with sharp claws, he became progressively more destructive in his "kittenish" growing-up habits. The furniture, curtains and anything in reach of the playful cub, took a beating. Tuffy soon outgrew the McNelly home and George took him out to his Red Lake ranch where there was more room for him to exercise without causing widespread damage.

George led him around on a leash, but always kept a watchful eye peeled for any indication of trouble. When January 1961, rolled around, Tuffy was about one-third grown. He accompanied us to Washington, DC, for the Presidential Inaugural Parade (our first inaugural trip). Tuffy's place in the parade lineup was in a cage which was hauled on a travois by a horse. The cub elicited considerable comment from the media and was the center of attention wherever he went with George.

In March 1961, two months after the inaugural trek, Tuffy was taken along on our regular rendezvous trip to Phoenix. We had the same setup as in the Washington parade; Tuffy, in his cage, rode on the travois. This parade was in bright daylight which made for more people seeing Tuffy as well as the mountain men; quite a contrast to the late evening gloom of that Washington parade.

Tuffy's home, after the Phoenix trip, was again at the McNelly ranch at Red Lake, He was usually tethered by a chain fastened to a tree in the yard. The long chain allowed for Tuffy's escape into the tree's branches above, should an inquisitive dog come too close for the comfort of the cat.

One day Tuffy disappeared. He had somehow broken a weak link in the chain and vanished. Two days later he was seen along

Highway 64 (Grand Canyon Highway) about twelve miles north of Williams—about three miles, as the crow flies, from the McNelly ranch. Presumably, he was searching for rabbits and other small game killed by speeding cars on the highway. He had never had the opportunity to put into practice the natural skills of hunting instinctively learned from infancy by his species.

Bill Williams Mountain Men

We again welcome the Bill Williams Mountain Men from Williams, Arizona. They are a group of civic minded citizens who have banded together to form a most unique organization to publicize their vacation land in northern Arizona. The regalia these men wear is made from the skins of animals that they have killed. Five days before the Rodeo, these men began riding their horses toward Phoenix from Willams. They rode all the way through mountains and desert, camping out over night on the way. A colorful group of men, good friends of the Phoenix Jaycees, and a welcome addition to this year's Rodeo.

A tourist stopped at a service station along the highway and reported seeing, as he drove by, what appeared to be a young lion that was just disappearing into a culvert under the road.

The service station operator, probably thinking about the bounty to be collected (business was slow), grabbed a rifle and drove up the road to the culvert. A look into the culvert disclosed the lion, crouched where he hoped was a safe refuge. A bullet dispatched the cat. The man hauled the animal out where he could get a better look at it. He then saw the collar. That collar around his neck identified Tuffy.

Several years later Tuffy #2 put in his appearance under much the same circumstances as had the original Tuffy—or Tuffy #1. Again George McNelly came into possession of a very young male lion cub and again took upon himself the monumental task of taming the cat into some semblance of domestic tranquility. George had the cage left over from his previous experience with Tuffy #1.

George succeeded remarkably well in the training program but he couldn't keep a constant eye on the cub. When the cub was in his cage unattended, kids, being kids with a natural streak of playfulness, spiked with more than a modicum of meanness, threw rocks and poked sticks between the bars of the cage at the lion. That quickly created in the animal an antagonistic opinion of the world in general and all kids in particular.

This second cat never became as trustworthy as had the original Tuffy. He was in a cage on a travois in one of our rendezvous parades in Phoenix. It was after that parade that Tuffy's downfall started. While transferring him from the smaller parade cage to a larger cage he was wounded by an iron bar in the cage gouging him in a shoulder in the process of the transfer. We had no way of doctoring him; we didn't dare get close to the deadly claws of the feisty cat.

That seemed like an ideal time to donate Tuffy to the Phoenix Zoo—they might be able to nurse him back to health again—they had the facilities and the know-how and we didn't. We hauled him out to the zoo and gave them the cat and cage.

Attendants at the zoo tried to get Tuffy back on his feet again and, for a time, seemed to succeed in their efforts but eventually they had to humanely put Tuffy to sleep.

It takes constant care to raise a wild pet. It is not just a temporary assignment where the project can be shelved to be brought to light only on rare occasions for parades, etc., and forgotten the rest of the time. No one in the club could take the responsibility or time to give proper care to another mascot—should the opportunity arise.

George McNelly had done an outstanding job of twice molding lion cubs into acceptable mascots and had twice seen his charges meet with disaster. He was of the opinion, and rightly so, that should anybody in the future desire to see the big cats, a zoo might well be the proper place to visit. As for the Bill Williams Mountain Men—Tuffy's #1 and #2 fulfilled their mission, but enough is enough.

Wagons Ho!

(what might have been!)

Several years after we had ironed out some of the wrinkles of the club's growing-pains, the appeal of nearby Grand Canyon again surfaced for discussion; we had briefly considered and discarded Grand Canyon as a terminus for the rendezvous trips in the beginning. The line of reasoning at that time was that the trips would not be long enough.

This time the thought was aired that instead of only a horseback adventure, we'd operate a wagon-train set-up with mounted outriders and the whole bit. This could be a plan that might eventually snowball into a full-fledged business—haul dudes from Williams to the Canyon at so much per head—make it a two or three day outing—circle the wagons at night—all the falderal of days of old—we might even stage an Indian attack. The ideas flew thick and fast.

This venture would in no way interfere with the already established annual rendezvous treks; it would be a separate adventure altogether.

There were, we were told, several miles of old military wagons stored end-to-end outdoors at Fort Bliss, Texas. Being out in the open and uncared for, they would soon be rusting and decaying. These wagons had been part of the armed forces equipment in years gone by, but were outmoded and no longer of use to the long-since motorized military services. They were sturdily built to withstand rough usage and would be ideal for our proposed project. All we'd have to do to complete the covered wagon motif would be to add the bows and canvas for the covers.

Doc Flohr, secretary of the Bill Williams Mountain Men at the time, corresponded with army authorities at Fort Bliss concerning the wagons, but not in time—we missed the boat. Some movie outfit beat us out. They bought all the wagons, spare parts, etc. We were left with only our dreams of what might have been.

In all probability we'd have been too old to operate the covered-wagon venture by the time we waded through the red tape involved in getting the wagons from Uncle Sam.

I think we all hated to admit that it was well that we couldn't follow through on the "covered-wagon caper." None of us had the time to devote to a pipe dream of that magnitude. We all had to work for a living and that didn't leave much time for indulging in another expensive hobby.

Mountain Men gather at Grand Canyon (l. to r.) Eddie Musgrove, Charlie Sharpe, Jerry Duffield, Gene Mason, Oscar Skaggs, "Doc" Flohr and "Spike" Way.

Potpourri

a "kind of therapy"

On our goodwill circuit of various hospitals in Phoenix, we went to Samuel Gompers Rehabilitation Center (when it was located on North Seventh Street) on several occasions. Once in particular, we trailered four horses out there. There was a large yard where the kids gathered to see us. They were mentally or physically (or both) handicapped, but all were anxious to be boosted up for a turn at riding around the arena on a real live horse with a real live mountain man. Many of them had never seen a horse before.

Our buckskins really got a thorough examination. We, of course, did not wear our knives—for the kids' protection and ours. Rifles, likewise, had been left behind (on occasion we did take along the guns which had been rendered inoperable). Once at a hospital, one of the kids grabbed a knife out of a scabbard and playfully (we liked to think) threatened one of his roommates with a promise to cut his throat. We, thereafter, tied the knives securely in our scabbards or left them at home when visiting the hospitals.

The kids' eyes sparkled as they crouched on the horses in front of a mountain man. In more than one of them, you could feel the little fellow's excitement as, in his imagination, he headed out at full speed to cut the bad guys off at the pass. After all, these kids had seen on TV how the hero always brought the culprit back to face justice. Some of them were good actors; they all enjoyed themselves.

As we left the Center that day, the supervisor told us, "What you did here today for our children did more for them than any kind of therapy we could have ever given them."

It did a lot for us, too.

Mountain Men (back row, l. to r.) Jack Munns, Bill Wilson, George McNelly, Ray Gardner, Jim Barber and Leo Black; (front row, l. to r.) "Spike" Way, Martin C. "Doc" Flohr, Louis Landry, and Thurman Mayes entertain the youngsters.

Cheering up a youngster at Good Samaritan Hospital are (l. to r.) Hurley Wright, "Spike" Way, Charlie Sharp and Gene Doyle.

"our hearts for Bumblebee"

Our third night camp of the second year's rendezvous was below Bumblebee, the same site as that of the first year. Everything was much the same as the first time around except that the natural pond down the creek had dried up and nobody expressed a desire to go swimming. We hauled water from the Bumblebee store. At that time the storekeeper invited us to camp there. He had corrals and lots of room for us. As we had already set up camp down the creek, we stayed at that location that night. The next year and for years thereafter we stayed behind the store in Bumblebee.

Early that night, several carloads of J. C.'s made a surprise, but welcome visit to our camp below the town. There was still lots of driftwood around, so we lit up the place with a large fire and had a big jamboree.

Bumblebee consisted of six or seven houses on both sides of

the road (old Black Canyon Highway) with a country store in the middle. In front of the store was an old-fashioned gasoline pump. We gassed up after helping the storekeeper manually pump the gas up into the glass bowl atop the pump. I don't remember what day of the week it was but we were the first gasoline customers that week. No doubt about it, this out-of-the-way place on the old Black Canyon route had seen busier times. Automobile traffic had come this way, following the old route of the stagecoaches, until I-17 was opened several years since.

Some time after our first overnight camp below Bumblebee, the entire town was bought lock-stock-and-barrel by a man from somewhere in the east. It's an ideal retreat for anyone wishing to get away from it all and it was a place where we always enjoyed making our night camp. We used their corrals

Phoenix Jaycees visit Bumblebee camp. In the foreground are a packrat-proof canister for food, Dutch ovens and coffee pot.

and were always made welcome.

We met some wonderful people while on our rendezvous trips. Once a man and his wife stopped along the trail at a noon camp to visit with us. They were temporarily living in Phoenix after having retired from a chicken-frying franchise they had operated in Michigan. They inquired as to when we would be at Bumblebee for our night camp. We informed them it would be the night after the one coming up.

When we of the cook crew reached Bumblebee on the afternoon in question, our newly-found friends from Michigan were already there. They were friends of the town's owner. They were setting up deep-frying equipment they had saved from their former business. They had stacks of refrigerated chickens that had been halved and par-boiled—ready for the finishing touch in the batter and deep fryer.

Talk about a feast that night—wow! No wonder we always had a warm spot in our hearts for Bumblebee.

in a "tie" at the rodeo

In our first few years some of the mountain men entered rodeo events as contenders, but more for their own entertainment. They competed in the wild horse race event for a couple of years and team-tying for several years. Thurman, Jake, Paul and Bill Lilly teamed up and entered the wild horse race event the first year we were there.

Those guys did more work and picked up more bruises in getting the saddle on that bronc than they had done in many months. They all said (except Thurman) that Thurman had the easy job, he—"got to go for a nice ride on that mild-mannered horse."

Thurman rode that bucking horse out of the arena after helping put the saddle on the animal, while dodging flying hooves and the tangle of human arms and legs. Easy job?—They did great but got no blue ribbon for their efforts.

Planning the trek are (l. to r.) Jerry Payne, Hurley Wright, Doc Stewart and "Spike" Way.

Thurman and Jake entered the team-tying competition in several rodeo performances. Considering the times being made by the professionals, if a contestant missed that first throw, he didn't stand much of a chance of finishing in the money. The mountain man team did well, but on one occasion, having missed the first throw, they went along with the entertainment—according to the press: "...the Mountain Men from Williams, with the dubious aid of the rodeo clowns, managed to tie down one of their horses instead of the steer—all in fun and adding to the enjoyment of the show."

"top scene stealers"

In one of the early years of the club's existence, KOOL—TV photographer Ralph Painter was coaxed away from his regular job to go along on one of our rendezvous trips. He made a full-length TV documentary, in color, of the group—the entire ride. Background music and commentary were dubbed in later. The film showed every phase of camp life: cooking, riding—the whole bit.

I don't know how many times Doc Flohr climbed in and out of his bedroll, alternately pulling on his buckskin pants and taking them off again over his long-handled red drawers; some of the time, the camera was pointed elsewhere, but Doc was giving his all to the picture. Doc and Paul Tissaw had somehow followed the wrong calling (up until now, that is). They turned out to be the top scene stealers. Someone less tactful might refer to them as "hams" but, damn nice guys to ride the trail with.

The documentary was trimmed to 25 minutes to fit a 30-minute spot on TV. We showed it to clubs, schools, Lions and Rotary Clubs. I've often wondered where that film ended up—it dropped from sight years ago.

"Doc" Flohr samples a birthday cake in his honor as Hurley Wright and "Spike" Way enjoy the occasion.

"frosting on the cake"

We put on a dance at Mayer one night while on one of our trips, in the late 1950's. We went by trucks and cars the few miles from our night camp, near Humboldt, to Mayer. The music was furnished by a string band from home (Williams). One of our members, Fred Theroux, was a member of the band.

The large dance hall was next door to Lonnie Wright's bar. Lonnie was a former inhabitant of Garland Prairie, near Williams. Lonnie's place was convenient for those who required proper oiling for the rigors of the dance. Sometimes a country dance can get wild, however probably quite tame when compared with a modern disco bash.

The bar and back-bar in Lonnie's place were genuine examples of the old classic furniture made in the 1800's. They were made of solid mahogany in New England and shipped "around the horn" (Cape Horn) by four-master sailing ship before the building of the Panama Canal. They were shipped to San Francisco, thence freighted overland by wagon to Prescott and finally to Mayer several years later.

A roistering crowd from Williams came down to join the local crowd to take in the dance. Everyone had a good time till well into the next morning. I doubt that the historic appeal of the bar was the sole reason for the crowd's frequent pilgrimages between the bar and the dance hall.

Oh, well, who needs more than two hours of sleep anyway? I don't recall our group putting on any more dances on any of our other trips. At least a part of a night's rest and sleep was deemed necessary to keep going in reasonable health. After the first couple of nights on the trip, almost everybody sacked out early and fervently hoped the late-carousing, but well-meaning visitors would pass us by.

As to the dance circuit: one year, a couple of nights after the competition of the rendezvous trip, the J. C.'s put on a dance at the Riverside Dance Hall in South Phoenix. They advertised that the Bill Williams Mountain Men would be there. We were there, although the money went into the J. C.'s fund; we were just frosting on the cake, as it were: a drawing card to get the dancing crowd out and we were happy to accommodate. The J. C.'s had been very good to us and we were glad to reciprocate.

Helicopter provides a backdrop for (l. to r.) Jerry Duffield, "Doc" Flohr, Oscar Skaggs, Gene Mason, "Spike" Way and Ed Musgrove.

the "clubhouse"

Somewhere in the first few years of our existence as the Bill Williams Mountain Men, the old Beacon Cafe went out of business. This place faced on both Bill Williams Avenue and Railroad Avenue. The latter was the entrance into the bar.

We decided to rent the bar section, closing off the restaurant. It would, we anticipated, make an ideal retreat or clubhouse. The bar was partially stocked—a part of a bottle of this—a part of a bottle of that, etc., which we bought. Glasses of only one size were left but we decided we could get along with a few glasses of one size; if nobody wanted too fancy a drink, we were in clover.

Shortly we broke in the place with a pot luck supper to

entertain our wives—a sort of "you're invited—you bring the food and we'll furnish the libation" affair. We all had a good time.

Another time this "clubhouse" was used was to entertain a visiting press correspondent from France. He had visited the Grand Canyon and had also included in his itinerary a visit with us to get a story for his publication in Paris. He said he had heard of our organization in France and wanted to see us in the flesh.

He spoke very little English—no problem—we had the "Frenchman," Louis Landry. Louie dusted off his long-unused French vocabulary and in a very short time they were conversing like a couple of long-lost friends.

About the time the second month's rent was almost due on the "clubhouse" the novelty of having the place was wearing thin. We had used the place for parties only twice and had been in the place only a time or two since then for a drink. It was more of a white elephant than we had anticipated. There was no incentive to pay rent on something we had little or no interest in. We moved out.

Even that far back (around thirty years ago) we were giving some thought about some day having a museum—some day— maybe, but we were not ready for a clubhouse.

"ride that steer"

Paul Tissaw trained a big bay steer to be ridden like a horse. He, of course, didn't take the animal on rendezvous trips, but occasionally rode him as a novelty. When the horses were trailered to different parades, the steer was sometimes taken along.

Paul and his steer were quite a novelty. They sometimes showed up in strange places—in bar rooms—dance halls— almost everywhere. Sometimes the steer would drop a reminder on the floor that he had been there. That didn't seem to bother either Paul or the steer, although it did impair their popularity in certain circles.

The *Sultana* in Williams and the *Palace* in Prescott were two of the establishments that somewhat reluctantly played host to Paul and his steer. At some time during a rodeo celebration Paul could be depended on to ride that steer or a horse into a bar. If he had been a mountain man at the time our original genre were active, he would have broken a buffalo to ride, "just for the hell of it."

"Spike" Way and "Diz" Dean entertain a passerby who wanted a picture with the Mountain Men.

"fun trips"

When we started taking guests along on our trips some of them didn't want to sleep on the ground; several took along pickups with campers attached. They did not want to "hob-nob with snakes and other crawly things," especially at night. We couldn't convince them that any self-respecting snake was still holed-up hibernating in early March when our rendezvous trek was under way.

That was not entirely a steadfast rule of thumb. One day a few riders were approaching the loading corrals near Sunset Point where we would camp that night. We had by-passed the Bumblebee route we usually went and stayed up on the mesa. The late afternoon sunshine was warm that day and, though a bit early in the year, a medium-sized rattlesnake had crawled out on a rocky ledge to sun itself.

Paul (who else?) played with the snake for a while. It was sluggish from its winter's sleep and not fully awake as Paul shoved it around with a stick. Tiring of the fun(?) Paul soon killed the snake with a rock, then picked it up by the tail and, even though his horse took a dim view of the proceedings, took the dead snake on to camp.

To say that Paul was a practical joker was putting it mildly; he played rough. Everyone around camp kept an eye on him, not knowing where that snake would turn up next. That night, when one of the men went to bed, he felt something cold under him. Somehow or other that buzztail had found its way into his bed.

The next day some of the horses and men found it advisable to keep a wary eye on Paul. He had the snake which he used as a whip to inject new life into some of the lagging horses. Horses and men have a common dislike for the sound of the rattles on a snake, dead or alive.

It was all part of the trip. Nobody complained—not aloud anyway; even in the face of hardship one seldom heard a discouraging word—strictly a fun trip.

Late in the afternoon one day in the Bradshaw Mountains, southeast of Prescott, a rain had been falling and had turned to freezing sleet. Ivan (Skipper) Robinette, one of the guests on the trip, was still several miles from camp (Skipper later became a member of the group).

The weather was freezing and there was no relief in sight. Skipper turned to his equally uncomfortable companion, Bill Sutton, and said—"you know, Bill, I feel like that monkey that was making love to the skunk—said the monkey—'I don't know how much more of this fun I can stand.'"

Yep—strictly a fun trip.

Rex Allen

Rex Allen was fast becoming famous in motion pictures and as a vocalist in 1956. His was the feature act of the J. C.'s rodeo that year. A great guy, a genuine cowboy and Arizonan.

"This is what Hollywood thinks a cowboy should look like," he quipped as he showed off his sequin-adorned finery in the arena. His horse, Koko, was one of the most beautiful horses in the business.

Marilyn Monroe

We saw Marilyn Monroe at the 1956 J. C. Rodeo. The Twentieth-Century Fox Studios were taking film sequences for "BUS STOP," a picture being made which starred the blonde actress. They shot some scenes of her at the rodeo arena.

She didn't impress us very much, except as a scrawny, under-fed female, not particularly attractive. Cameras and makeup artists sure work amazing miracles. The J. C.'s offered to give her to us to bring back to the mountains to fatten up; we declined the offer.

"silver miniature Mountain Men"

One day, Lloyd "Whitey" Nelson came into my office with a belt buckle. Whitey was a silversmith with few peers. This time he had a belt buckle he had just completed which he intended as a gift for Doc Flohr. Whitey had good intentions that day but he had not quite recovered from his latest encounter with *spiritis frumenti.* As he headed for Doc's office he suddenly succumbed to the thought—"just one little nip never hurt anyone," but he was broke. He made a detour from his originally intended destination, which brought him to my doorstep.

He was in need of his silversmithing tools which at the moment, he explained, happened to be in hock at a local pub—and—would I like to buy the buckle for $25 which coin of the realm would enable him to get his tools out of pawn so he could again pursue the vocation commensurate with his well-known skill.

That buckle was done in sterling silver, 2⅛"x3½" in size. It was an object of beauty and a classic example of the silversmith's art at its finest—a mountain man riding a horse and leading a packhorse stands out in bas-relief against a background of Bill Williams Mountain. The reins, bridle, halter, halter-rope, saddle, pack-saddle, long rifle, horses hooves—all were delicately engraved—truly a work of art.

Sure I would buy it. At that time I did not know the buckle was intended for Doc. Whitey later made buckles for Doc and several other members.

Shortly after the first rendezvous trip, Bernie Irwin, of Vaughn's Indian Store, informed us that their resident silversmith, Randall Honwesima, a Hopi Indian, had made a mold and could produce silver miniature mountain men replicas which would be made into bola ties. As soon as the first batch was made the mold would be destroyed (and it later was after the original, and only, batch was cast). These were intended to be only for the original charter members. Ten of the original thirteen members ordered and got our ties—if memory serves me right the cost was $18 per tie. This sterling silver replica was a little over two and a half inches tall, portraying a mountain man holding his long rifle.

Several years later, a new member borrowed a tie from someone (I never knew who). He, the borrower, took the tie to a Navajo silversmith friend over on the Navajo reservation. That silversmith copied the pattern by making a mold from the original, then cast some more replicas from the new mold. I guess that unethical practice was bound to eventually happen but somehow it didn't seem to be entirely right.

As time went by, we obtained smaller silver mountain men castings to wear on our hats; that would identify us, when not in buckskins.

"Old Bill's resting place"

Historians have a habit of shattering myths by digging out facts. Alpheus H. Favour and others carefully scrutinized Old Bill Williams' life, and death. They thoroughly and accurately pin-pointed the place and date of the demise of the old mountain man as being in Southern Colorado. The exact place of burial is unknown, but it is presumed to be near the place of his death at the hands of the Ute war party.

Before that discovery, legend was widespread that Old Bill was buried at the base of a massive rock pillar, high up on the Southwest side of Bill Williams Mountain. Friendly Indians were said to have, in accordance with his wishes, transported his body many miles after his death to this beautiful spot, now known as Bill Williams Monument or Chimney Rock. This impressive monolith stands nearly one-hundred feet high.

Chimney Rock, the Bill Williams Monument

Access to the site is by way of a little-used footpath that takes off from the road up the mountain, not far from the top. There is little to disturb the peace and quiet of the man who would want such solitude.

The thought processes of some of the old mountain men followed along the lines of the Indians of that time. They had the same superstitions. Some thought they would, after their death, come back in a different life as a bull elk or some other admired animal. Transmigration was more than a possibility in the minds of many of these men who lived close to nature.

Though Old Bill's resting place is far from his "monument" on Bill Williams Mountain, this site would certainly be to his liking. The solitude is unbroken except for the passing of an occasional wild animal or, an infrequent person whose curiosity is aroused by the indistinct trail near the mountain's summit.

Perhaps if one watched long enough and let his imagination stray, the spectral image of the Old Master Trapper might bridge the gulf of time and appear through the veiled mists of that dim trail on his way to another rendezvous... *quien sabe?*

"dream of a museum"

As this narrative was being written and published, the Bill Williams Mountain Men took the first steps toward realizing their long-held dream of a museum. Property was obtained at the northeast corner of Grant Avenue and Ninth Street in Williams and, in late 1986, four small cabins, originally built by the Fred Harvey company for the Grand Canyon hotel and tourist trade, were donated and moved to the property by Hal Nelson of Williams. As future time and money allows, these rustic structures will be refurbished to form the core of a future **Bill Williams Mountain Men Museum**.

Paul Tissaw on horseback glances back at "Spike" Way on the travois during a Winslow parade.

Epilogue

From a meager beginning with fourteen members, the club that started on not much more than a desire to get away from it all has developed into an annual pleasure trip—indeed, the club that was an experiment in adventure a third of a century ago has blossomed into an organization of national prominence.

The first trip to Washington, DC, in 1961 was perhaps the first taste of national fame that we were exposed to. Since our first invasion of the nation's capital, on Governor Fannin's invitation, the Bill Williams Mountain Men have made three more pilgrimages to ride in the inaugural parade.

The pioneering spirit that prevailed at the start is much the

Denton "Diz" Dean

Pete Miller

same as in years gone by. The horses are happy with their lot. Most of them get better care than when they are home.

Man, however, has become modernized; his comfort demands more attention. Many guests are taken along. Although the mountain men try to adhere to the old-time way of life (within reason), these guests expect more modern treatment than that rendered to the pioneers. Through it all, the camaraderie is still there. Everyone has a great time although once in a while the weather kicks up and hardships are incurred along the trail—everyone just buttons their coat a little tighter and enjoys it.

The Bill Williams Mountain Men is no longer a local (Williams only) organization. Long since, the original membership dwindled and the club was forced to extend the limits to encompass a statewide membership. Otherwise, things are much the same.

The cooking set-up has been modernized to an extent but the

Bill Lilly, one of the
original Mountain Men

Ben Fillmore looking for a horse to accommodate his pack saddle.

Dutch oven is still the dependable standby, available in case the modern conveniences fail. Perish the thought that these rugged old-timers should ever again have to rely solely on that old-time method of cookery—however, the mention of a Dutch oven somehow conjures up an aura of "roughing it" that fits in with the aims of the organization.

Libation dispensing methods have graduated or perhaps evolved upward from the "...pass the jug and we'll all have a drink" manner of the first rides. You won't see any fancy glassware, but don't be surprised if you are served up a "pink lady" or other fancy drink of your choice in a paper cup—or perhaps a tin cup? Naw, manners haven't evolved that far. The bartender isn't about to spend his time washing glasses or cups. You'll use paper or styrofoam and like it.

From the looks of things, the Bill Williams Mountain Men will be around for a long time as a reminder of a former way of life. So, grab a seat and watch the parade go by...get ready to cheer...and envy these hirsute and leather-fringed men from the mountains when they pass: they're probably on their way to rendezvous and to visit some kids in a hospital someplace.

Index

THE WEST

Discover arrowheads, old coins, bottles, fossil beds, old forts, petroglyphs, ruins, lava tubes, waterfalls, ice caves, cliff dwellings and other Arizona wonders. Detailed maps and text invite you to visit 60 hidden, out-of-the-way places. *Explore Arizona!* by Rick Harris (128 pages)...$5.00

Daring deeds and exploits of Wyatt Earp, Buckey O'Neill, the Rough Riders, Arizona Rangers, cowboys, Power brothers shootout, notorious Tom Horn, Pleasant Valley wars, the Hopi revolt—action-packed true tales of early Arizona!

Arizona Adventure by Marshall Trimble (160 pages)...$5.00

Guide to 38 of Arizona's charming and romantic small towns and hideaways. Visit such delightful places as Ramsey Canyon, Snowflake, Bowie, Window Rock, Wickenburg, Honeymoon and a host of other idyllic Arizona wonderlands. *Arizona Hideaways* by Thelma Heatwole (128 pages)...$4.50

Outdoor enthusiasts welcome this detailed guide to plants, animals, rocks, minerals, geologic history, natural environments, landforms, resources, national forests and outdoor survival. Maps, photos, drawings, charts, index. *Arizona Outdoor Guide* by Ernest E. Snyder (126 pages)...$5.00

THE WEST

Southwestern frontier tales more thrilling than fiction. Trimble brings history to life with humor, pathos and irony of pioneer lives: territorial politics, bungled burglaries, shady deals, frontier lawmen, fighting editors, Baron of Arizona, horse and buggy doctors, etc. *In Old Arizona* by Marshall Trimble (160 pages)...$5.00

Visit the silver cities of Arizona's golden past with this prize-winning reporter-photographer. Come along to the towns whose heydays were once wild and wicked! Crumbling adobe walls, old mines, cemeteries, cabins and castles. *Ghost Towns and Historical Haunts in Arizona* by Thelma Heatwole (144 pages)...$4.50

The American cowboy had a way with words! Lingo of the American West, captured in 2000 phrases and expressions—colorful, humorous, earthy, raunchy! Includes horse and cattle terms, rodeo talk, barb wire names, cattle brands. *Cowboy Slang* by "Frosty" Potter, illustrated by Ron Scofield (128 pages)...$5.00

Take the back roads to and thru Arizona's natural wonders—Canyon de Chelly, Wonderland of Rocks, Monument Valley, Rainbow Bridge, Four Peaks, Swift Trail, Alamo Lake, Virgin River Gorge, Palm Canyon, Red Rock Country! *Arizona—off the beaten path!* by Thelma Heatwole (144 pages)...$4.50

ORDER BLANK

Golden West Publishers

4113 N. Longview Ave.   Phoenix, AZ 85014

Please ship the following books:

____ Arizona Adventure ($5.00)

____ Arizona Cook Book ($3.50)

____ Arizona Hideaways ($4.50)

____ Arizona Museums ($5.00)

____ Arizona—Off the Beaten Path ($4.50)

____ Arizona Outdoor Guide ($5.00)

____ Bill Williams Mountain Men ($5.00)

____ California Favorites Cook Book ($3.50)

____ Chili-Lovers' Cook Book ($3.50)

____ Citrus Recipes ($3.50)

____ Cowboy Slang ($5.00)

____ Easy Recipes for the Traveling Cook ($5.00)

____ Explore Arizona ($5.00)

____ Fools' Gold ($5.00)

____ Ghost Towns in Arizona ($4.50)

____ Greater Phoenix Street Maps Book ($4.00)

____ How to Succeed Selling Real Estate ($3.50)

____ In Old Arizona ($5.00)

____ Mexican Family Cook Book ($5.00)

____ On the Arizona Road ($5.00)

____ Pecan-Lovers' Cook Book ($5.00)

____ Sphinx Ranch Date Recipes ($5.00)

Enclosed is $_____ (including $1 PER ORDER for postage and handling)

_____
(NAME)

_____
(ADDRESS)

_____   _____   _____
(CITY)   (STATE)   (ZIP)

This order blank may be photo-copied.

Bill Williams MOUNTAIN MEN

by Thomas E. Way

Send long, stamped, self-addressed envelope for catalog.